Shelter
NOW

We can count on a

world that has

learned and digested a

new idea of universality

and discretion in furniture,

literature, religion and music alike.

PAOLA ANTONELLI, MUSEUM OF MODERN ART, NEW YORK

8-00

shelter
NOW
creative ideas for today's home

NATALIA MARSHALL

with special photography by Chris Tubbs

contents

Introduction

"Funky" styling is a comfortable approach to home making, very much in keeping with the current spirit of globalism and eclecticism, so visible in our fashion, our food, and our music. Funky style defines shelter now.

Funky is a hybrid look; it combines the old and the new, the fun and the functional, the East and the West. It's about low-maintenance, relaxed, modular, and flexible living, where you can change a room's look and role by switching around your furniture or applying a new coat of paint. The ethos of this approach is that good interior style should be accessible to everyone, no matter what the budget. As such, it allows you to build on what you have, while adding items that will bring an inventive, fresh, and personal touch to your home. There's always room for excellent, classic design, but being funky also means embracing the kitsch, the witty, and the treasured ephemera of your life.

The funky look is closely aligned to fashion, where design innovations have slowed down, and instead new materials, finishes and fibers give re-invented styles a twist. Colors are bright and high-energy or muted and sludgy, and shapes are streamlined and organic, anthropomorphic and asymmetrical to enable you to make a bold statement in your living space.

In essence, today's home is a melting pot of happily unrelated items, picked up from markets, second-hand stores, trips abroad, collectors' fairs and art shows, or even made at home from interesting materials.

The key influences are the modern designs of the 1950s that embraced mass-production and functional forms, the geometric patterns and Pop Art of the 1960s, and the disco glamour and high-tech influences of the 1970s. The effect is that molded plastic and plywood seating with angular steel legs sit in acid bright settings with industrial-style metal or rubber flooring, and accessorized with bold patterns and glitter finishes. This creates a clashing aesthetic that breaks style barriers yet is totally compelling.

Key trends

There are a few key trends featured on the following pages that epitomize the best of funky, which can be used as a basis for creating your own highly idiosyncratic living space.

Harness the elements that appeal to you and don't be afraid to create new combinations with pattern and texture, shape and color. Customize anything you own that does not fit in with your fledgling look. The funky style seeker needs to be a jackdaw, a recycler, a repackager, a scavenger, and a shameless collector of anything that the less discerning interior decorator would pass over. Look for possibilities in anything unusual, old, discarded, or interesting. Use materials that are out of the ordinary, or use mundane materials in extraordinary ways. Traditional haberdasheries, hardware stores, stationers, "Asian" stores, and artists' shops can yield all kinds of effects from aluminum or bronze leaf to handmade paper, textured glass, and unusual or imitation paint finishes, to fabrics, ribbons, tissue, giftwrap, beads, buttons, and labels.

The look is certainly eclectic, but the end result should not be chaos. Although there are few rules, the practical advice in the pages of this book will help you achieve fusion rather than confusion. This is one style that can't be slavishly copied, relying as it does on adapting and customizing—and following your instincts. It is constantly changing, evolving, and modifying with you. So throw yourself into it, be creative, be confident, and, above all, have fun.

Modernity now is a bit like pop music—it's all about remix, taking an original, then redoing it in a new material.

FERRUCCIO LAVIANI, FURNITURE DESIGNER

Technological advances have introduced intense colors in lightweight plastics that inject vitality into the dullest of household objects. The theme is continued in wall paints and upholstery.

Hi-energy

plastic

polypropylene

acrylic

lime

tangerine

lemon

fuchsia

The enduring sleek, modern look of metal appliances and gadgets has been extended to the new metallic finishes in fabrics, paints, and wallpapers.

Metallic

aluminum

steel

chrome

zinc

bronze

pearly

glitter

reflective

shiny

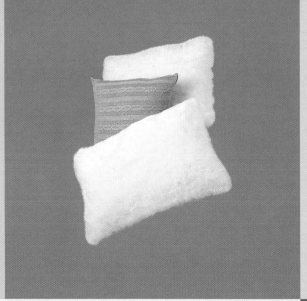

Sensuous and extravagant, fur (both real and fake) is stylish once again, and the longer the pile the better, together with anything bobbly, woolly, fluffy, and smooth. The funky home is filled with objects you just want to reach out and touch.

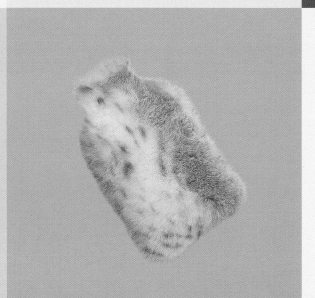

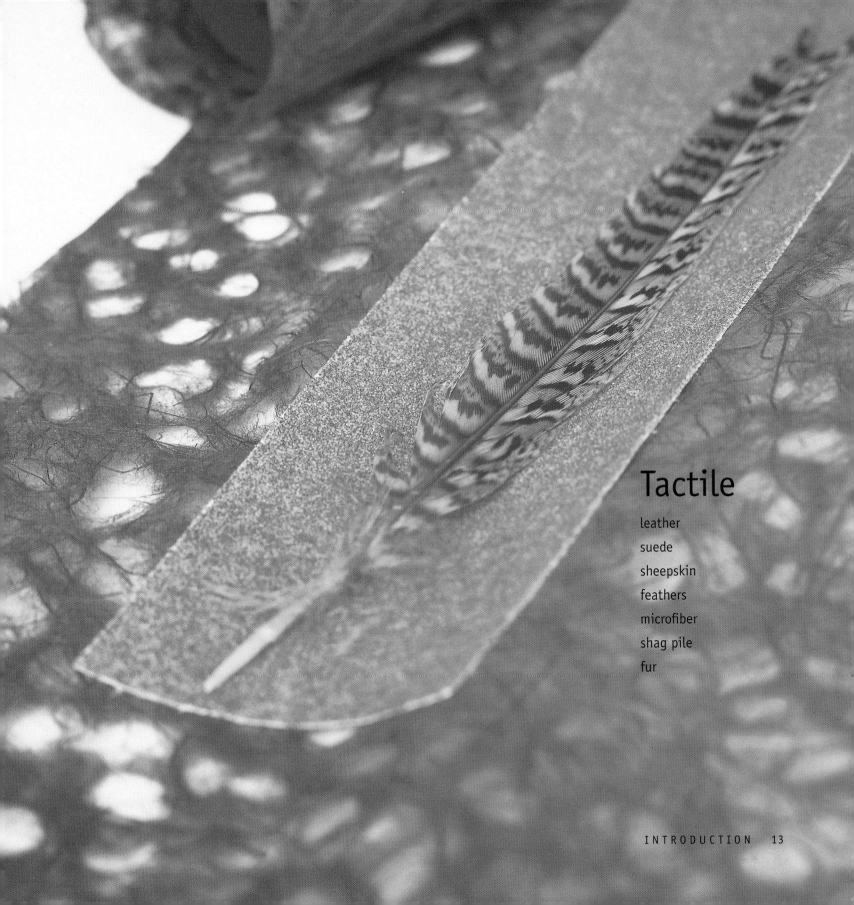

Tactile

leather
suede
sheepskin
feathers
microfiber
shag pile
fur

The sentimental and the gaudy can now be celebrated. Dig out your bits and pieces and display them with panache and humor.

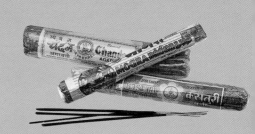

Kitsch

inflatables
fruit
Eastern
pets
pinks
embroidery
lanterns
imitation
cartoons
tassels

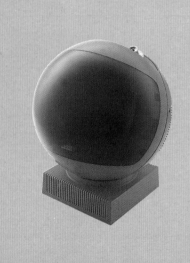

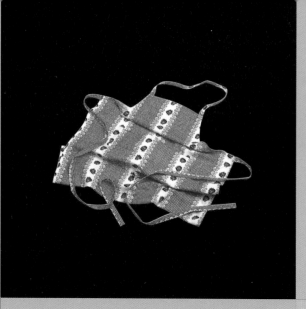

The popular and pioneering designs of yesteryear form the basis of funky styling, mixing genuine and imitation pieces.

Retro

circles

pop art

psychedelia

organic shapes

moulded plastics

chrome

geometric prints

leather

space-age

abstract art

gingham

color

Color sets the tone of the funky home, whether you want to head for the brash end of the funky spectrum in all-out primaries and acid brights, or create a restrained atmosphere, where baby blues and lemon yellows form a backdrop against which to show off the organic shapes of modern furniture and collections of accessories. Get ready to try chocolate brown, sultry beige, and serene grey—so long rejected as suitable colors for interior design. Now it's time to throw out all existing prejudices and try all sorts of new and exciting combinations.

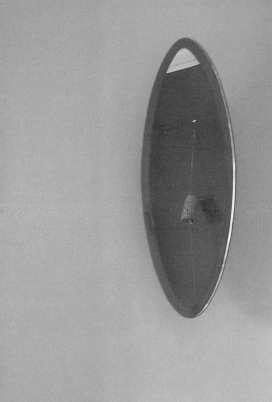

A Clever Color Scheme

Step into any good decorating store and you're confronted by row upon row of paint chips in every conceivable shade. Never has the choice of colors for the home been so varied and so dazzling, but the flip side of having so many tempting tones is that making the right choice can be a real challenge.

Glancing through glossy interiors magazines only adds to the confusion, crammed as they are with fabulous homes decked out in exotic shades of citrus orange and lime, purple, and—in these days of fascination with all things retro—beige and brown. It's inspiring when it's in other people's homes, but what about your own? How do you get that seemingly effortless color success?

As with so many other things, it's largely a question of choosing something that suits you, that suits your lifestyle—and furnishings, if you have them—and that creates the feeling you want from a particular room. But a little basic color science can go a long way in helping you get the balance right while achieving a truly individual look.

LEFT The citrus yellow-green of the walls here is accentuated by the raspberry wall lights and deep purple curtains. This scheme works because of the room's minimal and unfussy furnishings and accessories, mostly in muted colors, that really bring out the richness of the colors.

RIGHT This bold color scheme for a kitchen is uplifting despite the choice of a deep blue for the ceiling. Height is emphasized by the yellow and pale blue walls, and the unusual curved units help to break up the blocks of color, so that the overall scheme works brilliantly.

BELOW An injection of bright green provides instant impact in a hallway.

Setting the tone

As the largest surface area in a room, the color (or colors) you choose for your walls is crucially important when it comes to setting the mood for that room. A day with a paintbrush can transform a dull kitchen into a fresh one, or a gloomy living room into a vibrant one.

It's great to rifle through other people's ideas on color scheming, but ultimately what it comes down to is how certain colors make you feel—it's an emotional as well as a practical decision. For instance, wall-to-wall tangerine may make one person feel zesty and alive, but it may make a more nervous individual jittery or overwhelmed. The current mood for ecleticism is great, as it basically means anything goes (so long as it's done well and with the right accessories and furnishings). A little confidence goes a long way when it comes to combining colors, but if you need some help, most of the big paint manufacturers are now grouping their colors together in "moods," on the basis that any colors from one group will combine successfully, thus helping you to create a room that is either warm or cool, refreshing or vivid.

Where to start

Your starting point must be to assess what you already have in terms of furniture items or large accessories. If you have a sofa, a picture, a pair of curtains, or a rug you're into, try picking out one of the colors it contains as a starting point, and build up your color scheme from there. But make sure you know what kind of mood you're after. What is going to make you happy? Is it a room to chill out in, a room to be creative in, or a room to wake up and get energized in? Is it an adults-only room, or a family room? Will you use it mainly in the evening or during the day? The colors you choose will play a key role in generating this mood.

You also need to consider how light the room is. A bright, south-facing room with massive windows has a completely different feel than one that faces north or has tiny windows. In addition, at night, the kind of lighting you have can transform both the atmosphere and the colors (see Chapter 4).

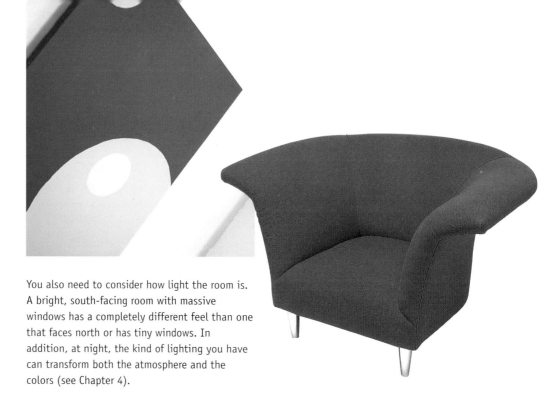

ABOVE LEFT Emulate the current art trend for things circular and have a go yourself using this simple abstract design. Try aubergine with acid yellow, orange with turquoise, cerise with lime green or coffee with cream. One sure guarantee of success is to use a gradation of tones, one of which matches your wall color. (See pages 34-35 for details.)

ABOVE A well-designed piece of furniture in a bold color is a good starting paint around which to organize your color scheme.

LEFT With colors like these, you really don't need much else in a room. This ultra-simple scheme works especially well because although two contrasting colors are used, they are similar tonally so one does not dominate. The turquoise wall color is continued over existing features, such as the tongue-and-groove panelling and picture rail, to maximize the sense of height and continuity.

Get it in proportion

When it comes to deciding how many colors to incorporate into your color scheme it is worth remembering that two colors used in exactly the same proportion can end up looking either busy or indecisive. So for a more fluid scheme, use just one dominant color to cover the majority of the wall space, and make up the balance with one or more shades. Other colors could go into the woodwork, on the ceiling, below the dado rail if you have one, or even on just one wall or an alcove, and be picked up in the furnishings and fittings.

A useful exercise when deciding on your dominant color is to rifle through lots of chips, narrow the choice down to a handful that truly appeal to you, and get tester pots for each. Paint generous-sized swatches on the walls, or paint large pieces of cardboard and move them around the room so you can see how the color looks in different lights. Don't make a final decision right away; live with your swatches for a day or two and see if you still like them. Put existing furnishings next to them and see how they go together—any serious clashes will show straight away.

RIGHT A restrained scheme of brown, cream, and maroon is warm and relaxing, but has a couple of twists to create interest. The alcove is painted in dark chocolate, a color that is repeated in the '60s-style fabric carefully folded across a thin pole to make the simplest of blinds.

Color combining

Once you've chosen your dominant color, you'll need to think about other shades—woodwork, for instance, the ceiling, or you may even opt for an above and below dado rail scheme. And this is the hard part: mix in the wrong shade and you'll kill your carefully chosen dominant color. One guideline that is easy to follow is to check that the tone and intensity of cohabiting colors match. If you're not sure about this, look at paint chips in the store. They are arranged not only by color, but also by the amount of black and white pigment that has been mixed in. So paler tones, the ones with the most white in, sit at the top, and the deeper, intense shades are at the bottom. Choose colors that come roughly from the same area. If you want to go all out for strong primary colors it is better to use not more than four, and use bright accessories as color accents.

ABOVE There are plenty of kitchen accessories that belong in the funky club. Just make them big, bright, and beautiful.

OPPOSITE This kitchen is full of glorious primaries, but there's enough pale wood in the units to keep it from becoming overwhelming. The combination works because the colors are all of the same intensity.

BELOW No kitchen should be without a cordless phone. Get one that matches your color scheme.

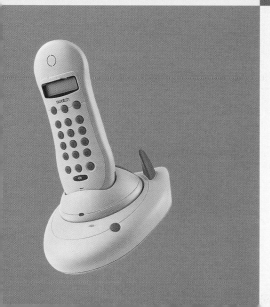

ABOVE Kitchen appliances can no longer be called white goods, when they come in such an astonishing array of colors and finishes, like this cobalt blue refrigerator.

LEFT Accessorize in a bright colorful kitchen with a yellow espresso machine.

Soft, challenging, or all-in-ones?

There are basically three ways of combining colors—contrasting, blending, and harmonizing. Contrasting color schemes are among the most exciting, although a certain amount of experimentation is necessary before it comes just right. Use colors that are at opposite ends of the spectrum, such as fuchsia with black and white, or deep purple with acid yellow. Blending, or monochromatic color schemes are easy on the eye and ideal if you find choosing colors difficult, as they use just one color as the basis. Interest is created by adding in graded shades of that color. If you want to be a little more adventurous, you could throw the whole thing into focus by introducing an accent color in tiny quantities: a chocolate brown cushion against lime green perhaps, or a crimson throw in a pale blue bedroom. Harmonizing color schemes are fairly straightforward to put together, and use two or three colors close to each other on the color spectrum. For example, you could combine warm colors such as yellows, ochres, and oranges or go cool with turquoises, blues, and lilacs.

Going white

White is not a color that is immediately associated with funky eclectic style, but it can provide a clean, fresh backdrop that will allow the dramatic shapes, bold designs, and luxurious textures of your furniture and accessories to take center stage. Try to avoid brilliant white, as this can look harsh, particularly in northern temperate zones. Instead go for off-white shades of chalk, eggshell, and beige.

Grey is another option that is becoming increasingly popular. Make a statement by choosing one or two cool grey tones for your walls and lifting the overall scheme with accents of shocking pink, luscious greens, and tangy orange.

Whatever color scheme you choose, it's best to rely on your own instinct. When all's said and done, it's as much about personal taste as anything. If a particular combination makes you feel good, throw all the rules out of the window and go for it. Be brave and adventurous, but above all go for something that gives you lots of positive energy.

OPPOSITE It doesn't have to be bright to be funky. In an all-white setting, attention is drawn to the mantelpiece and the quirky display of ephemera.

RIGHT Pale walls are the perfect complement to the minimalist feel of this urban living room, accentuating all the available light and space.

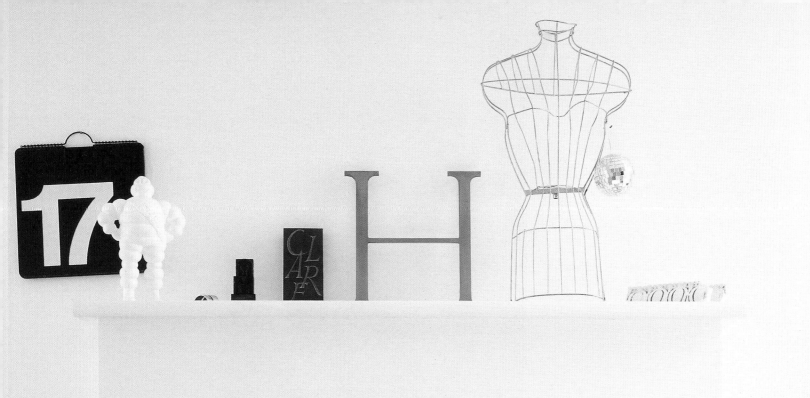

STYLE POINTERS

Choose colors that make you feel good.

Experiment with the biggest swatches you can get before you start painting. Remember that a whole room painted in a color is likely to appear around three shades stronger than in a tiny sample.

The amount and quality of light in a room affects color dramatically, so choose your color scheme according to the time of day that the room will be most used.

Generally speaking, warm colors such as oranges, reds, and yellows 'advance,' making a room feel smaller and more cozy, while cool colors such as greens, blues, and greys 'recede,' opening a room and making it feel more spacious.

South-facing and sunny rooms can get hot and stuffy in the summer. They can be 'cooled' with soft greens, aquas, or lilacs, or fresh shades such as lemon and fuchsia. North-facing rooms, on the other hand, lend themselves well to warm, vibrant colors such as honey yellow, terra cotta, and dusty pink.

Employ a little color psychology—colors have different wavelengths and affect our retinas in varying ways. Bright red has long wavelengths and requires our eyes to adjust a lot, so some people find a whole room in red claustrophobic. Green, by contrast, with its short wavelengths, is easy on the eye and restful.

Associations are important, too. Think of the openness of the wide blue sky, the relaxing power of the turquoise sea, or the warmth of a yellow summer sun.

RIGHT Take inspiration from your favorite movie or TV show. This red hallway's reminiscent of the dream sequence from *Twin Peaks.*

Dealing with problem areas

Few of us are perfect—we all have our own endearing quirks and imperfections—and the same is true of our homes. Many rooms are too narrow or dark, or are awkwardly shaped. And in the same way as you might change your hair color or apply your brightest and best Chanel lipstick, this is the time to think about using color to disguise those less-than-perfect characteristics. There are few rooms, no matter how strangely proportioned, that can't be helped by the right color scheme. Try some of the following solutions.

BELOW: Wake up each morning to a fresh, bright bedroom. Sorbet colors are invigorating and clean, and work well with a low-maintenance, easy-going room.

LOW CEILINGS
Use a pale color such as off-white or pale blue that will recede and make the ceiling seem higher. Contrast it with a darker color on the walls. You can also extend the wall color up into the cornicing if you have it, and down to the skirting board to make the walls seem higher, or paint architectural details such as dado and picture rails the same color as the walls to give an impression of continuity.

AWKWARDLY SHAPED ROOMS
You can use strong, advancing colors to alter a rooms' proportions; for instance, in an L-shaped room, paint the short and long walls opposite the same color to link them. Loft rooms with sloping roofs can look very odd and it can be hard to see where the ceiling ends and the wall begins. Get around this by painting the whole room in one color. Use vinyl silk emulsion paint as this has a subtle sheen that reflects light.

SMALL ROOMS
Painting a cramped room white is an obvious solution, but you could also try cool, receding shades such as violet, pale blue, or soft yellow. The same goes for the floor—choose a pale-colored floor covering and paint the skirting board in the closest matching shade you can find to make the floor area—and the entire room— seem larger.

NARROW ROOMS AND HALLWAYS
Make a room seem wider with strong, horizontal lines or patterns, ideally in warm, advancing colors. Try applying a lighter color below the dado rail level to create a horizontal line around a room and emphasize its width. Paint the two shortest walls the same advancing color so that they appear to 'meet,' while the longest walls should be in a pale, receding color.

circle artwork

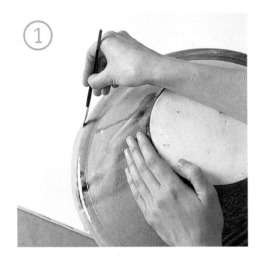

1 Place the bowl in the bottom left-hand corner of the canvas so that it cuts into the canvas as far as you want and paint around it using the lime green paint with a small artist's brush.

2 Along the diagonal from this corner to the top right-hand corner, place the cup within the painted circular outline. Paint around it using the apple green paint with the small artist's brush. Place the cup so that it cuts into the canvas at the top right-hand corner and paint an outline around this edge in apple green.

3 Paint the main circle with the lime green paint and allow to dry. Paint a second coat if required. Paint the two small circles with the apple green paint and allow to dry. Paint a second coat if required. With the larger paintbrush, paint the remaining canvas with the aubergine paint and allow to dry. Paint a second coat if necessary.

4 Paint down over the edge of the canvas by continuing the relevant colors using the small brush.

Materials

19³/₄ × 23⁵/₈in (50 × 60cm) ready-stretched canvas (available from art suppliers)
Large round bowl or plate
Small cup or jar
Small artist's brush
¹/₂in/1.5cm paintbrush

Tester pot of apple green (Dulux 0050-G40Y) water-based paint
Tester pot of lime green (Dulux 0080-G40Y) water-based paint
Tester pot of aubergine (Dulux 6030-R50B) water-based paint

TIPS Painting long, fast strokes gives a smoother line to the circles, but don't worry about getting the edges perfect—wobbly lines are fine. Wait until each circle is completely dry before doing the next to avoid blotching. Do a draft first on a piece of paper if you'd like. You can use any color combination, but to play it safe make one color the same shade as your wall, one a couple of shades darker, and one a couple of shades lighter.

paint effects

Committed funksters may well shudder at the words 'paint effects' as images of rag-rolling, dragging, and sponging spring to mind. But paint effects can be cool, as long as they are kept simple and clean—no textures please! Think of your interior walls as more than just somewhere to hang pictures. They are a canvas for your creativity, to be decorated in numbers, letters, circles, lines, and stripes in the new generation metallic, glitter, and pearlized paints. Break with convention, show some sheer audacity, and place them somewhere unexpected, in nooks and crannies, and incorporate existing architectural features. Try your hand with sample pots first, and if you feel nervous about the finished result, restrict your painting to just one wall. But draw them out with bold shapes; run circles around fireplaces and numbers around light switches. Precise symmetry isn't essential—play around with different angles, heights, and proportions.

Stripes

Horizontal or vertical stripes in the right place can be highly effective, but need to be done well —or at least assertively. Decorating books will tell you that horizontal stripes have the effect of making walls seem shorter, whereas vertical stripes make a room look taller, but if you limit yourself to pale colors, you should avoid much shrinking and expanding. Stripes in darker or brighter colors are enjoyed most by people who don't mind feeling dizzy and hemmed in.

If you have a fairly steady hand you could try applying the stripes by hand (draw them in pencil first), which gives a free-form, soft-edged look. Otherwise, and if your walls are sound, use low-tack masking tape to mark out the stripes. Use a spirit level to ensure they stay straight. If your stripes alternate light and

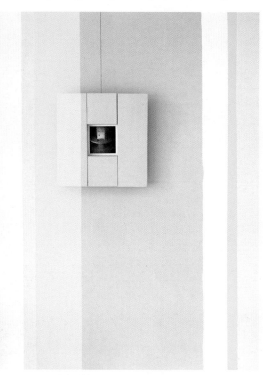

dark, you will find it easier if you paint the whole wall in the lighter color first, then paint the darker colored stripes over the top when the first coat is completely dry.

For a subtle and simpler effect, try a single horizontal band of paint in a different color than the wall that runs all the way round the room above the picture rail, skirting board, or at dado rail height. It can be as wide or as narrow as you feel is appropriate.

Blocks

Geometric shapes are so versatile because they can fit together to create an entirely new effect. A simple version of this involves painting each wall of a room in varying tones of the same color.

For a more dramatic finish on a wall that does not have a window, divide the surface into four or six blocks and paint each one a different shade. This can also be done on a smaller scale using colored squares or rectangles to make up a larger shape.

ABOVE Large screens painted in reflective paints have such a glorious, luminous sheen that little additional decoration is required.

LEFT Stripes in natural shades produce a pleasing asymmetry in a design that incorporates the picture frame.

OPPOSITE If you haven't got quite the right picture, make one yourself, by painting rectangles directly onto the wall.

Lines

A single line running either vertically or horizontally is very simple to do, yet can have a great impact. Create the illusion of a vertical line at the meeting point of two different wall colors half way along one wall rather than at the corner. Alternatively, use a dark shade to demarcate the meeting point of two paler colors. This device can act as a visual punctuation mark to divide two separate functions of a room, such as a dining or office area from a lounge area. The effect can be done just the same as for stripes, using masking tape, or if it's a thin line you want, you could just use one strip of tape, and use this as a straight edge along which to paint.

Letters & numbers

This is where you can get plenty of effect for the minimum amount of effort. You can make simple stencils by enlarging images on a photocopier and cutting out the shape, ideally with a scalpel for a razor-sharp edge. For extra strength, glue the paper stencils to cardboard and cut them out. Leaf through magazines or books from the '60s or '70s for some funky retro typefaces, evocative of childhood books and comics, detective and sci-fi novels, or take a trip to your local stationer or art supplier for contemporary stencils and Letrasets. If you have access to a computer, you can print out letters from its own supply of fonts and then enlarge them.

ABOVE Red and yellow meets and jostles for supremacy in a line that runs at an angle.

RIGHT Paint a random order of numbers with antique printers plates around the corner of a room, or pick out important dates such as anniversaries. (See pages 44-45 for details.)

OPPOSITE For the ultimate paint effect in a nursery or children's room, use dots to form letters of the alphabet.

Circles

Circles, such as those pictured on page 36, are quite time-consuming to draw out, but worth the effort for that evocative '60s feel. To achieve the same result, you have to measure out a grid on the wall using a pencil metal tape measure and spirit level. Covering a whole wall, and in soft shades, the end result is very satisfying. If you want to pursue a random arrangement, it's better to cover a smaller area. Small monotone circles running around a wall at skirting board height are mischievous and fun.

Metallic, pearlized, glitter, & fluorescent

For a touch of disco glamour, try dabbling in the frivolous range of metallic, pearlized, glitter, and fluorescent paints that are available today. You can choose from sugary pastels to luminous green or yellow, rich exotic golds to silver, bronze, and copper. You may not want to paint an entire room in these special finishes, but any of the paint effects previously mentioned would look very effective. Moderation is definitely the key to success. If you want to be really experimental, you could try covering part of a wall with silver or aluminum leaf, which comes in the form of sheets of rub-down transfer, usually sold in packs of twenty-five. It's a bit difficult to apply but can look brilliant.

1. Green hammered metallic

2. Fluorescent green

3. Blue glitter

4. Purple metallic

5. Gold metallic

6. Pink pearlized

7. Silver glitter

8. Silver metallic

9. Fluorescent yellow

10. Bronze metallic

11. Fluorescent pink

12. Cobalt blue metallic

stenciled numbers

1. Line up the spirit level at the desired height along the wall to ensure that you get a straight line.
2. Draw a faint line in pencil to act as a guide along the top of the spirit level.
3. Take a stencil and rest the bottom on the line. With a gentle stippling motion, dab the paint on to the stencil. Continue along the wall stenciling using the numbers and the paints in a random order.
4. When the paint is completely dry (in about 3 hours) carefully rub out the pencil line.

Materials

Tester pot of olive green
   (Dulux 3060-G90Y) paint
Tester pot of mustard yellow
   (Dulux 1060-G90Y) paint
Tester pot of red
   (Dulux 1777-Y81R) paint

Number stencils
Stippling brush
Ruler
Pencil
Eraser
Spirit level

TIPS The brush's bristles should be barely coated with paint and the stencil must be kept absolutely still to avoid ugly blobs. I used antique printer's numbers, but you could make your own stencils from stiff cardboard in small circles, squares, or other simple shapes. Avoid using primary colors if you don't want your room to look like a nursery.

flooring

The floor area offers great potential for experimentation and innovation. Carpet is quiet and indulgent, but there are so many other coverings available, many of which have migrated from industrial settings, that are practical and hard-wearing, and are perfect for the modern aesthetic. There are practical considerations, such as whether you have children and therefore need flooring that is especially hard-wearing and easy to clean, whether you live in an apartment building and need noise-absorbing underlay, or whether you already have wooden floorboards that are in good condition and need only a light sanding and varnishing. Virtually any kind of flooring lends itself to a modern look, depending on its treatment.

Funky floors

When it comes to home basics, what you walk on is just as important as what you hang your pictures on. It may be a cliché to say that the floor is the fifth wall, but it certainly does cover a large surface area and as such it needs a lot of attention and a lot of thought when you are considering the other elements of your interior style.

When you move into a new house or apartment, you may find yourself dealing with flooring that has been down for decades. Before you pull it up, check its condition. Linoleum that was laid in the '70s should still be in great shape, and is now considered the height of good taste. It may not be in the strong energizing colors of today's marketplace, but try to work with it rather than pulling it up.

Classic can sit happily with modern—the combination is a characteristic component of the funky look—so before you strip antique floorboards, or rip out elegant parquet or pale slate, consider how you can bring their inherent qualities into your funky style. Work them into your color scheme or make a design statement out of their worn appearance.

LEFT Old and new merge as a modern carpet is anchored over painted old floorboards with a metal trim.

RIGHT If you're lucky enough to live in a house or apartment that retains its original tesselated tiles and parquet floors, it is worth taking some time and effort to keep them looking good, as they provide a stunning backdrop to furnishings and accessories of any style.

Rubber

Rubber is probably the ultimate funky floor. It originally made its way into our homes during the hi-tech period of the late '70s, when industrial-style fittings were popular. If you want to pursue the more severe hi-tech look, opt for austere blacks and greys. These can act as superb foils for boldly painted walls. But if you're looking for something a little more cheerful, there is such a vast range of truly stunning colors available now that you could have a hard time choosing.

Rubber is excellent for kitchens and bathrooms, but true funksters don't stop there; they use it in living rooms and bedrooms too. It's warm and soft underfoot, it can be cleaned with a swish of detergent, it's hard-wearing and shrink- stain- and burn-resistant. It's antistatic (good for the home office), antibacterial, and when it comes to the varieties with raised textures of round studs, ribs, and grooves, are also antislip. It absorbs noise well, so it's perfect for party animals. Sounds too good to be true? Well, there's more: you can choose from plain, patterned, or marbled finishes, and if you can't find the exact color you want, you can have it specially made. As rubber is commonly sold in tile form, this gives you the added advantage of mixing your colors to create a checkerboard look.

LEFT When polished with a water-soluble wax emulsion, a uniform rubber floor takes on a beautiful glossy sheen with a heightened intensity of color.

Linoleum

Linoleum is making a big comeback due, to a large extent, to the fact that it is made from natural and sustainable materials (linseed oil, chalk, wood flour, and pine resin). Technical improvements have also increased the range of colors and patterns that are available. You can now choose from around thirty muted colors and a choice of decorative tiles and borders. It has a grainy matt finish, which can be buffed to a glossy sheen. Highly durable, antibacterial, smooth, and easy to clean, linoleum can be kept dust free with a quick swipe of the mop. It will improve with age, which in a funky home full of objects picked from the whole of the twentieth century is a plus. It's affordable, too, but should always be fitted by a specialist. One disadvantage is that it tends to come in fairly narrow widths, so large rooms end up with a seam running through it, but you can get around this by incorporating it into a pattern.

Vinyl

The notion of vinyl flooring may cause design purists to shudder, but it has moved on from the days of fake terra cotta tiles and strange abstract patterns—though of course these are still available if it's the retro '60s look you're after. Now you can find an astonishing range of finishes from specialist manufacturers, as long as you're prepared to pay rather more than for your standard vinyl styles, such as convincing imitation glass, marble, parquet, mosaic, granite, and metal. It even comes with disco-style glitter incorporated onto a background of colors such as mint green, lilac, silver grey, and midnight blue. Vinyl is washable, affordable, and easy to fit, although not as enduring as rubber or linoleum.

TOP RIGHT Made from natural yet highly resilient materials, linoleum comes in a vast range of dynamic colors and is deceptively warm to walk on.

Some types of flooring combine the warmth of carpet with the durability and cleanliness of vinyl, and are ideal for small children and pets. One of these is the product Flotex, which boasts 66 million nylon fibers in every yard, plus a waterproof backing reinforced by glass fiber.

We've been trying

to move on for 20 years,

then suddenly everyone

turns round and says,

hey we liked what was

happening in the 70s!

BARRY GIBB, BEE GEES

Metal

Originally considered suitable only for commercial and industrial settings, metal has become an acceptable domestic flooring. It has a sleek, eye-catching finish that is ideal for the industrial postmodernist look. You may not want it for your living room, but for kitchens, stairways, and even bathrooms, it can be very effective. Choose something with a raised pattern to protect against slipping. Metal floors are usually made from aluminum or galvanized steel, and have to be ordered from specialist manufacturers.

Concrete

Concrete is a flooring that is dismissed as harsh and unyielding, yet it can be instantly transformed through screeding and painting, waxing, or coating to achieve a stylish, shiny tone. Concrete can be bought as slabs or tiles, or it can be mixed and laid on sight. It is usually found only on basement and ground level as a subfloor. Simply pull up the upper flooring and check the condition. As long as the surface is not crumbly, chalky, or loose, you can use a couple of coats of ordinary emulsion or paint topped off with two or three coats of fast-drying acrylic varnish to give it a beautiful finish. As concrete is absorbent, the finished effect will be pleasantly faded. You can also use special floor paint, but it's not quite as environmentally friendly. If you do want to have a concrete floor put down, you could always embed other materials such as pebbles into it before it sets, then seal and wax it. If you are planning to lay a material like cork tiles over it, you will need to seal the concrete first with a PVA/water solution. Laminate and wood overlays won't require sealing, but if your floor is in the least bit uneven it will need to be smoothed with a liquid screed or a thin layer of plywood first. Keep concrete clean by scrubbing with hot water and detergent.

Carpet

Until recently eschewed in favor of hard floors such as vinyl and wood, carpet is experiencing something of a revival among the hip, the cold-toed, and the '70s wannabes. It may not be as hygienic and easy to clean as other kinds of flooring, but it is worth remembering its more tactile qualities—warm is now cool. There are plenty of varieties that meet the funky criteria. Shag pile, for instance, once deemed downmarket and surburban, has been rediscovered by advocates of '60s style. Deep and luxurious with a pile of up to 2 inches long, a shagpile rug in shades of chocolate brown or cream is an essential item for any funky living room.

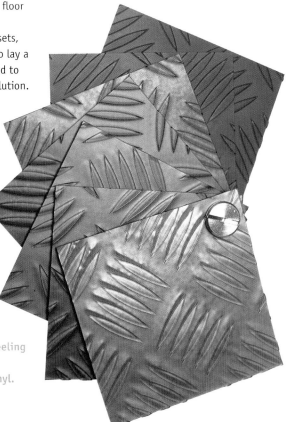

Color addicts can look for carpet in such shades as turquoise, orange, and citrus yellow. Add a border in a contrasting shade or perhaps an animal-print pattern for added zing. Ideally go for 80 percent wool mixed with 20 percent manmade fibers such as nylon for the right blend of durability and softness. Then there is the range of natural fibers of sisal, coir, jute, and rush that are chosen for their muted shades, loose weaves, and nubbly texture. Carpet is not great for damp areas such as bathrooms, so if you're determined to stay soft underfoot stick to carpet tiles.

ABOVE Break down boundaries and bring the garden inside with a 3-D effect imitation floral rug.

BELOW Introduce an instant splash of color to an otherwise monochrome floor with rugs in abstract patterns.

Sanded floorboards

The simplest and most affordable of all floors, stripped and sanded wooden boards are universally appealing and versatile, and can be done by hiring a floor sander over a weekend if your existing boards are suitable. Add a jolt of color with a groovy rug, treat them with a muted color wash, or go minimalist and simply apply a few coats of clear acrylic varnish.

Strip wood & laminates

A vast expanse of floor shimmering with light-colored wooden flooring looks terribly sophisticated. If you can afford it, solid wooden floors such as ash, oak, or beech will last for years and are easy to maintain. If you're on a budget, a good-quality laminate (thin strips of wood glued onto other materials such as plywood) can look good, too, but don't expect

too much durability—the surface coating tends to wear away after just a couple of years. Wooden floors can also be fitted over a thin layer of insulation, ideal if you need extra sound-proofing or warmth. For the ultimate funky wooden floor, you could paint a shape directly onto it as an imitation rug or to demarcate different areas. (See following pages for details.)

ABOVE The natural grain of stripped floorboard brings a understated vitality to this kitchen that is mirrored in the muted pattern of the animal print fabric covering the bar stools.

LEFT Laminated floorboards provide a sleek modern look that can be dressed in any number of ways.

OPPOSITE Plain floorboards are given the funky treatment with a zebra print rug.

circle floor effect

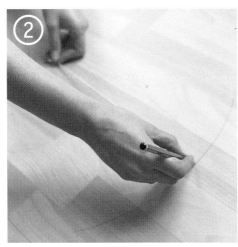

1 Knot the end of a ball of string around a drawing pin and, holding the pin lightly in the floor, unravel the string to the desired diameter of your circle. Cut off the length of string and, holding it tightly, test the size of your circle.

2 Attach the pencil to the end of the string. Holding the drawing pin down firmly with one hand, draw a circle with the pencil.

3 Lightly sand the floor surface within the circle to provide a key for the paint.

4 Carefully paint within the pencil line in red paint. Allow to dry. Paint a second coat if required. Paint a topcoat of protective water-based varnish to protect the surface.

Materials

Bright red emulsion paint

Medium-sized paintbrush

Sandpaper

Water-based varnish

Pencil

Ball of string

Drawing pin

TIPS Draw the circle in one fast, sweeping movement. I used ordinary emulsion paint, plus a protective topcoat of clear fast-drying varnish, but you could also use special floor paint. You can paint a circle onto concrete or wooden floors; concrete needs to be sealed first. Floorboards that have already been varnished need a thorough sanding and cleaning with methylated spirits before you start painting.

lighting

Lighting is usually thought about right at the end of the design process, long after all the other elements have been put into place. But this is a mistake, as good lighting can wonderfully enhance an already successful color scheme, and poor lighting just as effectively kills it. Imposing floor lamps and stunning chandeliers can provide great focal points, soft accent lighting can alter the mood dramatically, while projected kinetic lighting is the modern answer to firelight—a flickering, ever-changing light to bring life into a room. So do yourself and your home a favor, and think about good lighting early in the design process.

Flexible Lighting

When it comes to lighting, it's all too easy to run into a trendy store, grab a few lamps, then plug in, switch on, and chill out. All well and good, as far as it goes, but there are smarter ways to approach one of the most important aspects of home design. Stick to a few basic rules and make your lighting really work for you, enhancing moods you want to create, highlighting favorite objects, creating a sparkling focal point, or simply providing light to live, play, or work by.

There's nothing worse than a powerful bulb right in the center of a room that casts its unforgiving glare all around and provides absolutely zero atmosphere.

By contrast, the most successful lighting schemes are usually the ones with most flexibility, and this applies to any interior style. Get the lighting right and your room is made—get it wrong and your carefully chosen color scheme is lifeless. Versatility is key, so install as many dimmer switches as you can, have plenty of portable table lamps, and in dining/kitchen areas have the central pendant light on a long flex so that you can extend it and lower it over the table when you have friends to dinner. Introduce the funky element through colored bulbs and quirky shapes in your lampshades and bases. There are essentially five different kinds of lighting to think about: ambient, accent, task, decorative, and kinetic.

ABOVE Just like a doll with different outfits, this little cylindrical design comes with several different paper sheets that can be changed to suit your room. It's the ultimate flexible lamp.

RIGHT Make your own lampshade out of polypropylene that provides an effervescent glow when lit. The detail is added in the rivets that hold the shade together. Make several in different colors as the perfect finishing touch to a mellow atmosphere. (See pages 68-69 for details.)

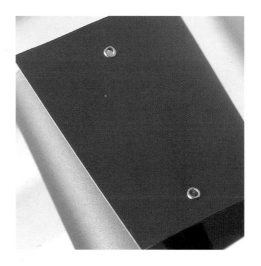

RIGHT Add a touch of glitz to your home style with a glorious chandelier. This version mixes colored with clear glass for a truly glamorous look.

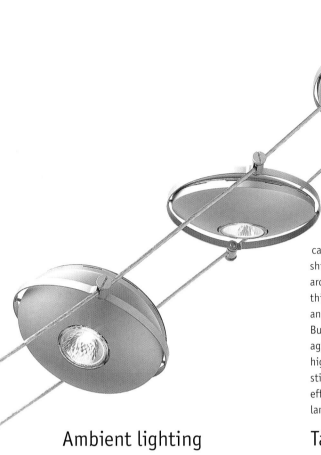

Accent lighting

Once your ambient lighting is in place you can install low-key accent lighting, which can shine onto pictures, plants, ornaments, or even architectural details such as recesses. Done well, this creates interesting shadows and reflections, and breathes life and atmosphere into a room. But it's not simply a case of sticking a lamp up against your finest Warhol reproduction: only highlight things that are really worth it, and stick to just a couple of accent lights for greater effect. Try recessed ceiling spots, angle poise lamps, and adjustable spotlights.

Ambient lighting

Ambient light is the light that surrounds us, and forms the basis of lighting design. During the day, ambient light comes naturally from windows and doors, and at night it should come from a bright but well-shielded source, ideally a combination of wall lamps or up-lighters (small, low-voltage fittings set into ceilings or walls), or, failing that, an overhead ceiling light. You should aim for workable brightness, but avoid anything that gives off glare. Where possible, create a softer feel by directing lights against walls, floors, and ceilings. Dimmer switches are useful for creating the right mood, too.

Task lighting

Task lighting isn't just for the home office—you need it for everyday jobs such as cooking, reading, or writing letters. Ideally, task lighting should shine onto the area you are working in or on, highlighting detail, but it shouldn't be so bright that it makes you wince. Find task lights that are adjustable, have shields around the bulbs, and have reflectors or lenses to cast light in the direction you want. If you work at a computer, use a 60-watt-bulb—anything less can cause eye strain. For the kitchen, fit adjustable spots with dimmer switches that can focus on different activities such as eating or cooking. Position strip lights under wall units to reduce glare.

Decorative lighting

A truly fabulous ceiling, wall, or floor lamp can create such a wonderful focal point for a room, that little else is required. Decorative lighting may not be as practical as other kinds, but when you've got a shimmering crystal chandelier, a giant white obelisk, or acid-bright plastic cones to admire, who cares? If you can't afford to buy a stunning lamp, it's easy to make your own with a favorite ornament or customize one you already have to make it a bit different.

Kinetic lighting

Kinetic lighting (from the Greek "to move") is purely frivolous. It is moving light that brings energy and movement into a room. Kinetic lighting comes in the form of flickering neon lights, amorphous glitter or lava lamps, or simply from twinkling candles and dancing firelight. You can even hang a revolving disco ball and shine light onto it for a sparkling mobile reflection.

WHICH BULB?

Before you buy a light make sure you know what kind of bulbs it uses. Tungsten bulbs are the most common but they have a short life span and are not very energy efficient, although they are affordable and cast a familiar, yellowish light. Fluorescent bulbs, including the compact kind, are energy efficient and long lived, but can cast a very bright and artificial light and cannot be dimmed. Low-voltage halogen bulbs are reasonably energy efficient, dimmable, and give a clear white light that's fairly close to natural light. The bulbs are small and fit into unobtrusive light fittings; however they can be expensive. If you buy a light that requires an unusual size or style of bulb, buy a few spares at the same time to save you trouble later.

ABOVE If you need soft, warm lighting for a bedroom or living room, opaque glass globes like these are simple yet elegant and stylish enough not to need a shade.

RIGHT This inflatable plastic cone light makes use of colored light bulbs, which you can change to alter the mood in a room.

Get the Right Light

Pendant lights

Back in the '80s the pendant light was seen as the poor relation to more sophisticated sources such as recessed ceiling lights, but now that designers have realized that not everyone wants to take on the financial responsibility of a whole new system, they have returned to this old trooper introducing a wealth of interesting new designs to make these lights popular once again. Many rooms have just one central ceiling light that can become a focal point, so choose a lampshade that's funky as well as functional. Models that direct light upward give a much softer light than those with exposed bulbs.

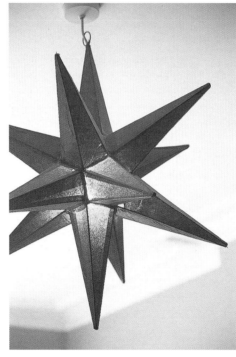

RIGHT Unconventional materials and shapes characterize funky lighting.

LEFT Colored dots are never far away in the funky home. Introduce them into your design scheme on translucent plastic.

Table lamps

No room should be without its full quota of table lamps, the most flexible kind of lighting. You should buy a size that fits the proportions of your room, and remember that the taller the lamp base, the wider the pool of light it casts. Dark shades tend to absorb light, while pale shades reflect it. Shades made from opaque materials such as plastic or card tend to give a directional light, casting shadows up or down (good for task lighting), while translucent shades made from paper or glass give a softer glow (better for ambient or accent lighting).

Standard floor lamps

Freestanding floor lamps are indispensable sources of ambient, task, or accent light, and their height can add a welcome variation to low furniture. Translucent shades are best for ambient lighting, and opaque for accent or task lighting. Choose lightweight, easily portable lamps for extra flexibility. A rigid standard lamp is good for up-lighting walls, while flexible designs are better for reading or other close-up work.

Up-lighters/down-lighters

These are lights which direct light either up or down, and can be wall-mounted, freestanding on the floor, or fixed onto track systems. Up- and down-lighters are good for highlighting special objects or creating a specific atmosphere.

Opposite: Disguise ambient lights as pictures. In this apartment, exuberant flower designs are lit up from behind as the light is projected through the colored glass.

Right: The artichoke lamp is made from translucent white plastic, and its offbeat design guarantees its standing as a focal point.

Do you have enough?

The worst thing you can do is under-light a room. It may cost a bit more at the outset, but invest in good lighting—and plenty of it—and you'll have the means to change the atmosphere from warm and relaxing to bright and energizing at the flick of a switch. Unless your living space is very small, try using some of these lighting recipes as your lighting ideal.

LIVING AREA
One pendant light
Two to four up-lighters
Three or four table lamps
One or two decorative lamps
Two picture lights

OFFICE/WORKROOM
One pendant light
One standard lamp
Two table lamps
One or two task lights

BEDROOM
One pendant light
Two bedside lights
Two wall lights
One or two table lamps

LEFT Funky lighting can be discrete. This dining room gets plenty of natural light during the day, and a couple of simple wall lights are all that is needed to set the tone at night.

RIGHT A slim, pretty string of tiny paper boxes is an attractive alternative to the standard reading lamp and gives a lovely diffused light. Their versatility of form allows you to drape them, hang them, hide them, or coil them to suit yourself.

STYLE POINTERS

Small rooms can look larger and more spacious with a couple of up-lighters to bathe the walls with light

Install dimmer switchers, especially in bedrooms and living rooms.

Don't ignore natural sources of light; candles and firelight add drama and warmth to your lighting scheme.

If you work with a computer at home, make sure light shines on the keyboard rather than at the screen. Position the computer with its back to the window (and use adjustable blinds) to reduce glare.

If you use a dressing table to make up, install table or wall lights on both sides to evenly illuminate your face.

Read with the pendant light dimmed low and a lamp shining directly on to your book.

Just a couple of sparkling white halogen lights will inject any room with a touch of glamour.

Use small light bulbs for strong atmospheric shadows, and pearlized bulbs for a soft, more diffused light.

If you like the idea of flickering light but don't want the conventional style of a candle, try this cute red candle man instead.

polypropylene lampshade

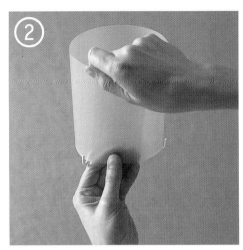

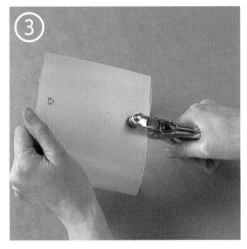

1. Cut out a rectangle of polypropylene to the length and width required to suit your lamp base.
2. Bend the polypropylene around the spider to test the extent of the overlap and ensure the shade sits firmly on the feet.
3. Holding the overlap firmly, remove the shade and rivet it at the top and bottom to secure.
4. Place it back on top of the spider, tucking one of the feet inside the overlap.

Materials

Sheets of polypropylene
Standard rivets
Rivet tools
Lamp spider
Lamp base
Scissors

TIPS If you're not confident about cutting the polypropylene immediately, or wish to try some unusual curvy shapes, experiment first with a paper template. I used a simple spider device, but you could also use a standard lampshade frame. With polypropylene, the more intense the color, the less translucent it is when lit. Make sure you always use a low-wattage bulb, as higher wattage will melt the polypropylene and ruin all your hard work.

pattern
& texture

Using various pattern and textures is a good way to express creativity and bring excitement into your home. This is the point at which you can add shape and dimension to your living space, creating points of interest and defining your personal funky style. On the walls, sofa covers, curtains, throws, blinds, chairs, floors, and of course, accessories, you can introduce as much or as little as you like. The aim is extravagance: animal prints and strong geometric patterns are all dominant features. Indulge yourself with luxurious fabrics such as velvet, mohair, chenille, feathers, brocade, and embroidery, and experiment with the designs of new and synthetic textiles.

Using Pattern & Texture

The repetition of patterns and touches of texture bring depth and movement to a room. Ideally these elements should come after you've chosen the main color scheme, unless you already have something you can't bear to part with, in which case you could use it as a building block of the room's design scheme. Soft furnishings are an obvious place to introduce patterns. There's no need to coordinate everything in sight, but it's a good idea to have some kind of a game plan, choosing small areas of detail that are similar in color or tone.

Patterns

Start by keeping things fairly simple, with perhaps just one or two patterns. You can always add to them later. If there's nothing you like more than a riot of crazy patterns and rainbow colors then go for it—as long as you don't mind the risk of over-stimulation.

If you already have a highly patterned carpet or sofa, it might need to be calmed down with a plain wall color. If on the other hand you have indulged in paint effects on the walls you may choose to have plain soft furnishings and create interest through texture instead.

Get your use of pattern in proportion. Large-scale prints can dominate a room and make it look small, while a large number of small patterns can look lost and insubstantial in a large room.

If you are not yet confident about using patterns, restrict their use to small-scale items such as cushions, stools, and throws that can be moved around till they find their right place.

Make use of an obvious color scheme to link different patterns, or make use of one pattern in two or three different colors to bring a unifying element to quite a bold pattern scheme. The aim is not to overwhelm but to add interest and vitality.

Above all, get those swatches in. Beg, borrow, or buy the largest possible samples and try them out alongside existing features and paint colors.

ABOVE Boldly patterned rugs create a splash of drama, and these black and white numbers from Ikea interconnect, too.

RIGHT A modern version of the Butterfly chair, which contrasts a tactile, fleecy covering against the pattern of its angular metal legs.

Funky patterns

If you'd like something completely original, rummage through lengths of retro fabrics at markets and car boot sales. The abstract geometric shapes of the '50s and early '60s in muted shades work surprisingly well with contemporary color palettes. If you want something more offbeat and colorful, try late '60s and early '70s psychedelia to set your pulse racing. If you don't want to use these fabrics for large-scale curtains or sofa coverings, cut and sew them into generously sized cushion covers, stool tops, and table runners.

If you're unlucky in your quest for originals, make your own—Pop Art–style designs work especially well. Much of Pop Art centers around strong, bright, patterns such as cartoons, or recolored photographs, so you can design your own piece of plain fabric with repeated images of your choice. Some large print shops can transfer these images onto the material (look in the Yellow Pages). The images may not be completely washable, so restrict their use to decorative blinds (laminate them so they can be wiped clean), wall hangings, and throws.

If you like the idea of a genuine '60s look, you could get in some fabric dyes and wax and try your hand at batik, or simply get knotting and experiment with tie-dye, both of which work well on curtains and cushions.

LEFT A colorful paper wallhanging can cover blemishes on the wall, adding a uniform pattern in a degradation of color.

ABOVE RIGHT Repetitive patterns of a single image or circles and other geometrics are very funky.

RIGHT Florals are acceptable in funky style as long as they are not too pretty.

Fabric

Natural fibers such as cotton and wool are wonderful and versatile textures to have in your home, but now that we are embracing all things synthetic and retro, man made fibers such as nylon and acrylic are making a big comeback, alongside innovations such as suede-effect microfibers. And let's face it, they do have some solid benefits such as being colorfast and washable. That's not to say that silk, cotton, wool, and linen should be forgotten—they still form the backbone of most people's soft furnishings, but these can now be supplemented with rubber, astrakhan, and plastic. Opposite are just a few examples of the best of modern fabric.

Wallpaper

Contemporary walls are looking sophisticated and tactile, and wearing shiny, glittery, and pearlized surfaces, fake wood and bamboo panels, hessian, weaves, leather, and suede effect, offbeat stripes and checks. It's hard to forget the shiny sponge-clean vinyl, strangely surreal florals, and ugly wood-chip that gave wallpaper a bad name, but the new designs and textures present a very different story. There's plenty of retro wood-effect and textured wallpaper around to please '70s revivalists, but alongside them come more modern interpretations featuring hand-painted designs, magnificent prints, and futuristic photographic images. The bad news is that the best of modern wallpaper is fairly labor intensive to produce and it can be expensive, and there's still the battle of the trestle table to contend with. Still, for a touch of character and individuality in part of a room, perhaps on just one wall or an alcove, it could be a worthwhile investment.

HI-ENERGY
1. Tangerine chenille.
2. Lime chenille.
3. Fuchsia corduroy.
4. Pea green Chinese silk.

METALLIC
5. Glittery plastic.
6. Disco synthetic.
7. Bronze metallic.
8. Shiny tortoiseshell plastic.

TACTILE
9. Red matt rubber.
10. Brown textured cotton.
11. Pink astrakhan.
12. Fake snakeskin.

KITSCH
13. Shiny nylon.
14. Organza-covered feathers.
15. Pink floral plastic.
16. Overblown silk Chinese motif.

RETRO
17. Circles and roses.
18. '70s squares.
19. Homely cotton.
20. Organic patterned cotton.

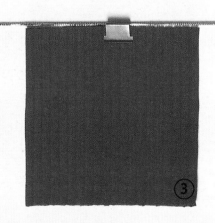
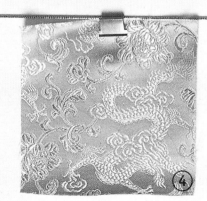

ABOVE Go on, be a hedonist. Soft, fleecy, and knitted cushions in a harmonious blend of colors look great and are lovely to touch.

TOP RIGHT There's no reason for stools to be neglected. Have them re-covered in imitation fur just like these.

ABOVE RIGHT Stepping out of a sci-fi movie, the Bubble Chair looks wacky and can give you a massage too! Add a softer element with a quilted throw in cotton, satin, or silk.

Texture

Anything tactile is a good alternative to pattern, and if you can mix different textures together for a luxurious layered look, so much the better. Cross the fluffiness of sheepskin with the warmth of knits, and the soft sheen of velvet and suede in blended colors. Keep your eyes open as well for furnishings in mohair, leather, chenille, corduroy, and nubbed woollens and silks. A fur throw is a must. (See pages 80–81 for details on making one yourself.) If you don't want to go for real fur, then there is a range of fake varieties available that creates a similarly glamorous look.

Funky style is about mixing and blending different textures to tantalize the senses, so get carried away by contrasting plastic bubble placemats against the surface of a polished wooden table, and smooth stainless-steel units against the raised relief of a metal floor. Place the luxury of natural fibers like cottons and silk satin alongside mass-produced furniture from manmade materials.

Colors are important too, when you consider that there are wonderfully energizing dyes for fake fur fabrics, so that you can avoid their natural look altogether and pick something totally synthetic. Feathery throws in acid pinks can conceal an old sofa under their softness and help bring an otherwise aberrant piece of furniture into your room's scheme.

RIGHT A medley of different textures and colors makes for a fun yet sensual feel in a room, through the contrast between the thick pile of the fake fur rug, the downy feathered appearance of the pink throw, and the smoothness of the plastic table. Satin textiles add extra titillation.

Mixing pattern & texture

Create startling opposites and contrasts through your use of patterns and textures in furniture and soft furnishings, and maximize the potential of both in everything you have. Consider the inherent pattern in objects and furniture and juxtaposition of accessories. The raised texture in a metal floor, for instance, creates a rhythmic pattern, and soft patterns appear in fur as they catch the light and are moved by your hand.

For a really chic look go for combinations of texture, such as smooth and rippled, fluffy and metal sleek, to add a sensual quality to your home. Alternatively be inventive with one type of pattern and incorporate texture. The circles in a blind can be mirrored in the texture of the Bubble Chair, or a bobbly rug or mat. Similarly color can create differentiation on a theme, so that while the pattern you have chosen may be wild and funky, the effect is satisfying and calming.

The picture on the left shows sumptuous use of these two elements of home style. Pattern emerges through the contrast of the strong circular outline of the table set against the more delicate swirls of the accompanying chairs. A curved edge is also echoed in the shape of the sofa. Rich Eastern colors help to lift the overall scheme and the black and white prints of the cushions covers add a visual punch.

STYLE POINTERS

Don't use paint effects such as sponging or dragging to introduce texture to your room—they are definitely out of style.

Try a limited amount of the new-look wallpapers in metallic, glittery, pearlized, textured, or geometric finishes.

Experiment with swatches before using more than a couple of different patterns in one room.

Indulge yourself with as many different textures as you like—go for velvets, fake fur, feathers, fleece, knits, weaves, and chenilles.

Scour secondhand shops and markets for good retro-patterned fabric that could be made into a blind, wall hanging, or even laminated placemats.

ABOVE A taste of the Orient is mixed with exotic colors for these funky cushions.

LEFT Elements from the natural world are brought together in an attractive way. The animal-print candles sit comfortably beside the handcrafted vase and bowl of pebbles.

fake fur throw

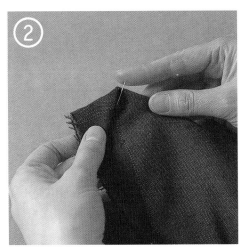

1 With the velvet right-side up, fold the fabric at one of the corners to bring the edges of two sides together. Working back from the corner, place pins at the point where the fabric is $1^{1}/_{2}$in (3.5cm) across.

2 Fold the velvet along this line and pin where it touches the fabric. Machine or hand sew along this line and trim off the excess material. This will give a velvet trim of an inch, plus a seam allowance of half an inch. Repeat steps 1 and 2 with the remaining corners.

3 Line up the straight edges of the fur and velvet exactly along one side. Machine sew along this edge. Repeat for the three remaining sides, catching in the edge of the corners; leave a small opening along the fourth side.

4 Turn the throw right side out through the opening and smooth out the corners. Close up the opening with neat overhand stitching.

Materials

56in (1.4m) square fake fur
60in (1.5m) square of velvet
Thread
Sewing machine
Sewing kit

TIPS I used a thick-pile fake fur, but short pile such as fake astrakhan, pony print, or zebra would also look good. For the trim, felted wool, textured cotton, or suede-effect microfiber are all good alternatives. The size of the corners dictates the width of the velvet trim, in this case an inch. It's important to get this part right; the rest will follow naturally. When sewing the seam across the corners, make sure the fabric is neatly tucked down flat to avoid ruching.

windows

Today's pared-down styling embraces the clean, the smooth, and the streamlined, allowing windows to do what they should be doing: letting in light, air, and sunshine. Funky window dressing can still be colorful and even dramatic, and there is always room for gorgeous curtains, but avoid tie-backs and frilly ruching. Sheer fabrics in white or jewel colors, full-length curtains in stunningly patterned or textured fabrics, café-style half blinds, severe metal blinds and shutters, glass bricks, and decorative finials in materials such as glass, copper, resin leather, or steel can breathe life into the most ordinary window.

Window styling

Windows are important both in the architectural framework that they bring to a room and also in the way that they allow natural light to filter into the room, uplifting the spirits of all who sit inside. In an ideal world, where privacy is not an issue, and cold winter nights don't make us want to draw inside and shut out the world, we would leave our windows unadorned to accentuate their shape, possibly painting them in a shade of the wall color. But the treatment of your windows through structure, pattern, or one of the other methods mentioned in this chapter can allow you to be as creative with the windows as you are in the other elements of your home's style. If you don't know where to start, make sure your blinds and curtains fit in with the rest of the room's theme. Coordinating them with the color of your walls or the upholstery is a reliable starting point.

Ready-made curtains

Ready-made curtains are affordable and easy to source and fit, especially the kind with tab tops that you simply slip over a curtain pole. Don't skimp if you go for this option—curtains that are at least one-and-a-half times the width of your window. Buy them too long rather than too short, as any excess can always be draped artistically over the floor or even chopped off to make cushions. If you do have to shorten them, leave a wide deep hem that will add a little weight to the bottom of the fabric, helping it to hang smoothly.

LEFT A louvered blind echoes the design of the cupboard door for a cool modern bathroom.

Where there's room, fit a curtain pole that extends a reasonable length at the sides to accommodate the curtains when they're pulled back. If you like to add your own imaginative touches to plain ready-mades, you could sew points of interest such as eyelets, buttons, beads, raffia, tiny bells, shells, or anything else that catches your eye. If you like quite a dramatic look for your windows, use two-layered curtains for extra versatility. The thicker layer can be drawn back in the summer. Add subtle character to full-length curtains by sewing two or three horizontal pleats near the bottom.

Make your own

If standard fabric curtains aren't what you want, try some of the following simple and cheap alternatives.

Make your own blind from any kind of funky fabric, or rubber or plastic (see pages 74–75), perhaps in an interesting shape, then have it laminated so it stays that way.

Use fine muslin or other sheer fabric to keep out prying eyes but to let in the light.

If the idea of sewing makes you queasy, find lengths of groovy fabric and, fold over a hem,

ABOVE These full-length curtains boast a wild pattern that is picked up in the circular pattern of the rug, while the floor cushions bring a whole new meaning to the word coordinated. Not for the fainthearted, but it makes a tremendous impact.

LEFT A draped dark blue curtain frames the window and merges with the blue of the walls and window recess for a contemporary look. Blinds are pulled down for privacy.

and press it flat, and attach to your curtain pole with curtain clips.

Try putting a tall screen next to a window instead of curtains or blinds.

Dye good-quality cotton sheets in bright, high-energy colors and hang them up with curtain clips for an easy modern look.

Buy lengths of silk or even saris and drape them over a pole for a luxurious and exotic look.

If you want to make your own blinds, linen, hessian, and canvas don't necessarily need lining.

If roller blinds are your choice, add detail with a pelmet made from the same fabric or in a contrasting color, and trim the edges with a narrow border in a different shade.

Use steel mesh (the kind for screen doors) as a shiny metal blind. Tuck in any sharp edges and simply pin it neatly to the top of the window frame, using steel or aluminum pins.

If it's flat, you can make a blind from it. Sheets of wood veneer, millinery straw, handmade decorative paper, sheets of MDF, strips of bamboo, sheets of Perspex, or even giant leaves can all be strung up from a piece of dowelling or pinned to a pole with clips. Encase them in an opaque fabric such as organza if you like, or have them laminated.

Make your own simple curtains from lengths of muslin or organza and add pockets of Perspex to color the light coming in. Hem the sides and the top, and sew at the top to thread through curtain wire or dowelling, or use curtain clips. (See pages 90–91 for details.)

If you're making curtains for the first time remember to make sure the pattern and warp and weft run in the same direction on both curtains.

CURTAIN POLES

Curtain poles don't have to be wood—wrought iron, glass, bronze are all effective, and can be topped off with decorative and colorful finials.

For a cheap and cheerful curtain pole, spray a broom handle with metallic brass or copper paint or use a length of piping.

As an industrial-style alternative, replace conventional poles with high-tension steel wires. You can then clip on your blinds with clips or even safety pins.

LEFT Sheer sari fabric looks beautiful, lets in light, and can be easily draped over a simple curtain pole.

RIGHT Hang your hand-made curtain with peg rings over a Perspex rod.

Alternatives

ETCHED GLASS

The easiest way to customize plain windows is by turning them opaque with a special etching spray, available from hardware stores. Make your own stencil (letters, patterns etc.), stick them lightly to the window, and spray over the top with several coats of etching spray. When completely dry, carefully remove the stencils to reveal the clear glass motifs on a stylish frosted-glass background.

SIMULATED FROSTED GLASS

Get a sophisticated sandblasted effect by sticking

self-adhesive frosted film, available from stationers and print suppliers, over your windows. You can cut out your own pattern using a scalpel.

Stick tracing or tissue paper over the glass for a colorful and opaque effect. Use strips of different colors for added interest, or paint on a pattern with metallic paint.

STAINED GLASS

Make your own stained glass. Draw on a simple pattern with indelible marker pen and cover it with ready-to-stick window lead, which comes in an easily dispensable roll. Paint each section with colored glass paint.

Alternatively, you can simply draw your pattern onto a sheet of acetate the same size as your window, paint with black outliner that comes directly from a fine-nozzled tube, and fill in the pattern with glass paint. Attach the sheet to the window with spray-mount adhesive.

Another way of creating a colorful stained-glass effect is to use long-lasting self-adhesive sheets of vinyl (available from specialist suppliers), either translucent or opaque. Clean the window thoroughly with methylated spirits and allow to dry before peeling off the backing paper from the vinyl and sticking it onto your window.

GLASS BRICKS

Glass bricks, once jealously guarded by builders and architects, have now become freely available to the creative public. They provide a wonderful alternative to ordinary glass windows, lending a functional modernity that is also immensely practical: they are tough, durable, and easy to work with. Because they really are bricks (typically about 3 inches thick) and hollow in the middle, they offer great insulation from cold, heat, and noise. Standard glass bricks are square,

THIS PAGE Window treatments include self-adhesive vinyl, glass bricks, and metal shutters.

SHUTTERS

Shutters are a great alternative to blinds or curtains. In addition to being immensely stylish, they let the light in when folded back, help keep out the cold or heat, and offer good security when bolted. You can have them made to order by a carpenter, or large hardware stores sell the components ready to paint and hang yourself. Alternatively, try salvage yards and second-hand shops for period shutters—look out especially for the louvered kind with slats that open and close to keep out the cold (and nosy neighbors). Half-height shutters have the advantage of letting in the light during the day while maintaining your privacy. If you fancy making your own, wood or MDF are good materials, or try Perspex, which is easy to work with and comes in lots of different colors.

transparent and very affordable; for a few more bucks you can get your hands on dazzling colors such as turquoise, pink, red, cobalt blue, pale green, and yellow in different sizes. A few enterprising bathroom and kitchen suppliers sell glass bricks with interesting textures such as ripples, bubbles, and waves, and patterned or opaque finishes.

You could try replacing a conventional window with a solid panel of glass bricks, although this requires a certain amount of know-how about things such as load-bearing and waterproofing. If you're not exactly handy with a tool kit, then cheat: simply pile up an assortment of glass bricks on the window sill so that they fit across the width. You don't need to place them the full height of the window—halfway up is plenty. Choose different colors and sizes for an abstract effect and place colored glass vases on top. Admire the light as it shines through the different colors and pools on the floor or ceiling.

LEFT Hang a glass beaded curtain at the window to keep out prying eyes, yet let light shine in.

stained-glass blind

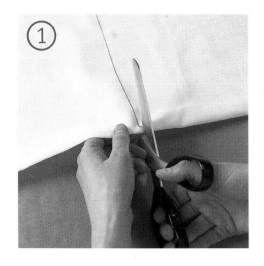

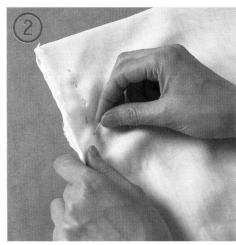

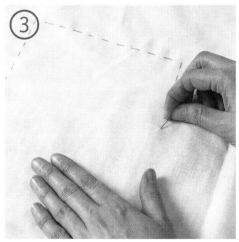

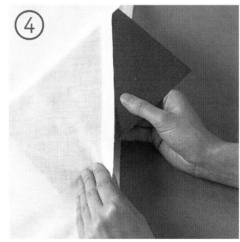

1 Cut the muslin so that when folded in half with the selvages running down one side, it fits the width and drop of the window with a $\frac{1}{2}$in (1cm) seam allowance.

2 Working on the reverse of the fabric, pin the cut edges of one side of the muslin together, starting about an inch down from the fold. Machine sew a neat, straight seam along this edge and along the bottom of the blind. Turn the fabric the right way. Press with a warm iron.

3 Cut rectangles of colored polypropylene to the size of your choice and experiment with their positioning on the surface of the blind. Then mark the pockets with tacking thread. Sew three-sided pockets through both sides of the fabric with invisible thread. Remove the tacking thread.

4 Tuck the polypropylene rectangles into the pockets, entering the blind through the selvage. Insert hooks in the window frame and hang the blind by pushing the dowel through the fold in the fabric.

Materials

Muslin to fit window
Colored sheets of
  polypropylene
Scissors or stanley knife
Sewing machine
  or sewing kit
Invisible thread

Dressmaker's chalk or pencil
Ruler
Iron
Small decorative hooks
Length of dowel for
hanging

TIPS Use postcards, dried flowers and leaves, sheets of fluorescent or hologram card, and festive decorations or small flickering lights at Christmas as alternatives to the polypropylene. Use pure cotton muslin (rather than a polycotton mix) for a crisp, clean look. Use a stiffening spray for a more rigid effect. The muslin needs to be sheer enough to be translucent, but strong enough to bear the weight of the inserts of polypropylene.

furniture

Furniture may provide places to sit and lounge, but just as important is the style statement it makes, and every piece you own ought to say something loud and clear. It is worth remembering that the desirables of today are the collectibles of tomorrow, so the design ethos of funky furniture is key, whether you buy new or second-hand. Shop for reinvented or original twentieth-century classics—designs that were considered progressive in their day. Hunt out items with shiny steel and aluminum frames, chrome trims, moulded plastic, seasoned leather or plywood seats, or select modern bulky shapes in hi-energy colors to create a powerful focal point in your lounge, dining room, or bedroom.

Funky Classics

Funky furniture takes inspiration from the fun and the functional, and embraces both updated classics in modern materials and innovative new styles that break all design barriers. The quality (and therefore the longevity) of design is important, and it is very telling just how much of the furniture today first made its way into our living rooms back in the '50s, and '60s. The funky look is connected to the modernist movement of the '20s, postwar utility styling, and the experimental designs of the '60s. The elaborately carved wood, cheap pine, stuffed upholstery that were popular until recently have given way to more understated, streamlined designs that have their origins in the machine age revolution.

Look especially for cultural icons—furniture designs that broke new ground in materials, principles, and techniques—from the big names of the twentieth century such as Alvar Aalto, Ludwig Mies van der Rohe, and Le Corbusier of the '20s, Arne Jacobsen, Charles and Ray Eames, Eero Saarinen, and Robin and Lucienne Day from the '50s, and Gaetano Pesce and Verne Panton of the '60s. If you can find (and afford) an original item, so much the better, but as mass production has given everyone access to quality design at affordable prices in a way that would have gladdened the hearts of Charles Eames *et al.* there's no excuse not to be funky. Stick to the following classics, and you can't go wrong.

RIGHT This stacking chair of 1960 was the first one-piece, cantilevered, moulded-plastic chair. It was designed by Verner Panton, a Danish architect and designer famous for his space-age, futuristic, curved chairs, sofas, and lights.

This modern sofa harks back to the '50s, when the first mass-produced furniture was simple yet organic in design and economical to produce—a departure from the cumbersome look of the prewar years.

Asymmetric, streamlined designs in shocking colors, such as this elegant sofa, characterize the funky look.

LEFT One of Ludwig Mies van der Rohe's most celebrated furniture designs, the Barcelona chair (on the left) was first made in 1929 for an eponymous exhibition and is still made today by Knoll Associates in the U.S.

The design of the *Ant* chair, first produced in 1950–51 by Arne Jacobsen, has encouraged many imitations, including this modern interpretation. The Danish architect and designer is best known for his designs using the new and exciting materials of the '50s: moulded plywood, aluminum, and fiberglass. The *Egg* (see page 92) is another best-seller still in production.

The *Grand Confort* armchair is a Le Corbusier design. This radical Swiss-born architect was arguably the most influential and revolutionary designer of the twentieth century. Working in Paris during the '20s with his wife, Charlotte Perriand, he produced many furniture designs that have become icons. Look out also for the B301 with bent tubular steel frame, calfskin seat and back, and slung leather arms, and the ergonomically designed B306 chaise-longue, both of 1928.

One of the first designers to produce organic designs, Finnish Eero Saarinen is famous for the Tulip table (1955–56). Originals were made in moulded fiberglass, but modern updates are often made from metal or wood. The table is accompanied by chairs with the same characteristic single pedestal foot: Saarinen's objective of the design was to clean up the 'slum of legs' in domestic interiors. Both this design and his Womb chair stand as landmarks in furniture design.

It may not look comfortable, but this Mexican chair certainly looks great, and its form evokes the welded steel rod construction chairs of Charles and Ray Eames and Harry Bertoia.

Inflatable chairs first came into fashion in the '60s, and are a good solution to providing extra seating in a hurry. This black version is stylish too.

The Balzac armchair and ottoman (1991) is indicative of the work of British designer Matthew Hilton, which marries modernist principles with traditional furniture-making techniques. This piece is named after the French author Honoré de Balzac, whose work explores the relationship between society and the human condition.

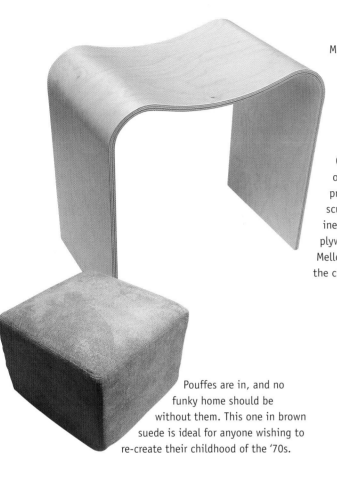

Moulded plywood became a popular material for furniture after aeronautical industry experiments during the Second World War. It was pioneered by Charles Eames, among others, in an attempt to produce organic, sculptural shapes inexpensively. This birch plywood stool by Corin Mellor is a modern take on the classic idea.

A perfect design to fall back on, the ubiquitous brown leather armchair can adorn any setting, whether modern or period, and exudes connotations of comfiness, reliability, and style.

Pouffes are in, and no funky home should be without them. This one in brown suede is ideal for anyone wishing to re-create their childhood of the '70s.

A contemporary design that hints back to the organic shapes of the '60s, this coffee table has plenty of practical storage space—and it looks fabulous.

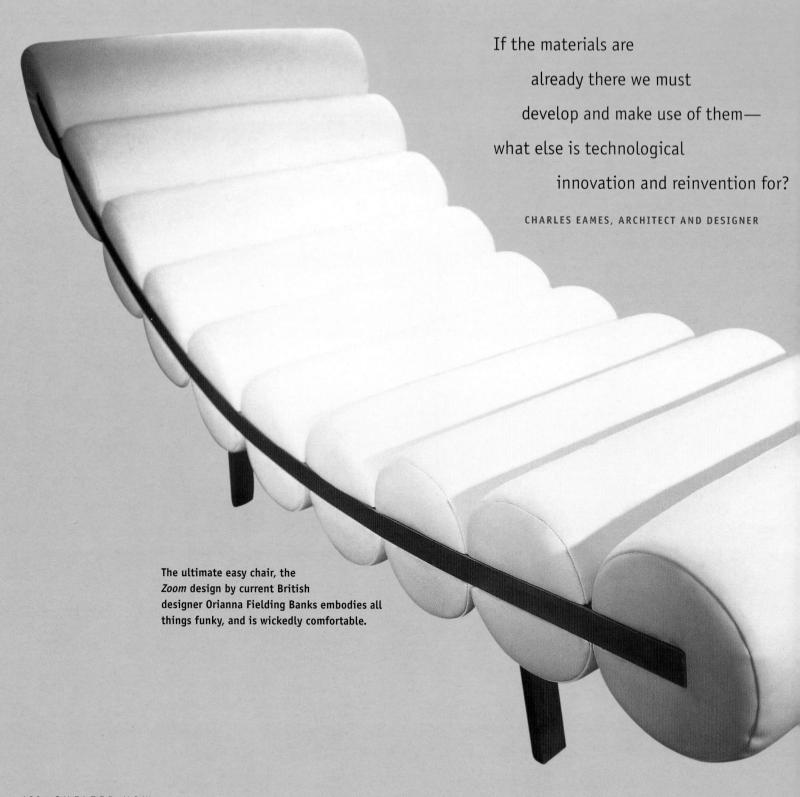

If the materials are already there we must develop and make use of them—what else is technological innovation and reinvention for?

CHARLES EAMES, ARCHITECT AND DESIGNER

The ultimate easy chair, the *Zoom* design by current British designer Orianna Fielding Banks embodies all things funky, and is wickedly comfortable.

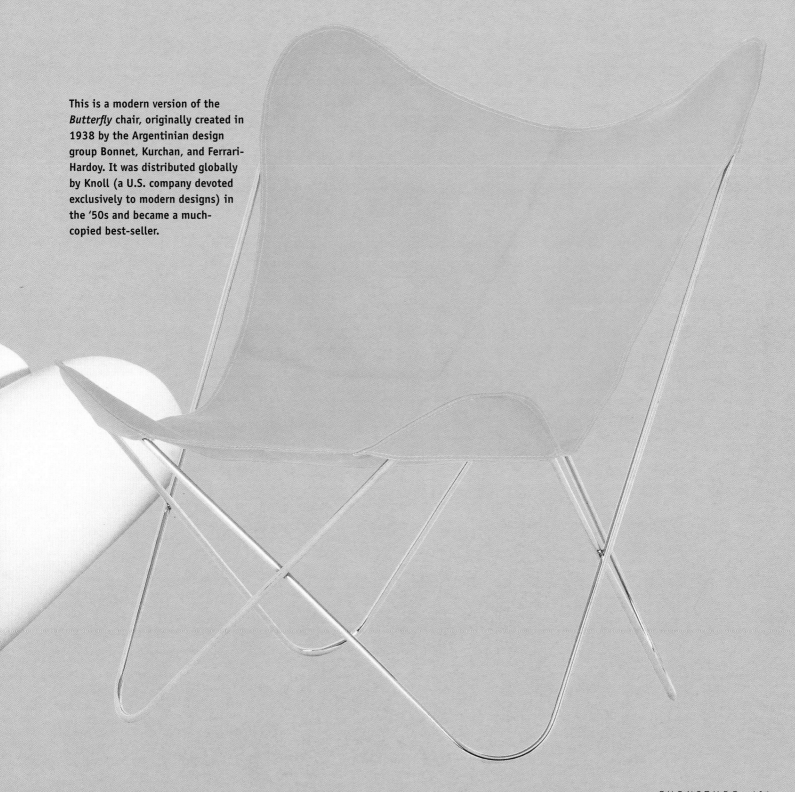

This is a modern version of the *Butterfly* chair, originally created in 1938 by the Argentinian design group Bonnet, Kurchan, and Ferrari-Hardoy. It was distributed globally by Knoll (a U.S. company devoted exclusively to modern designs) in the '50s and became a much-copied best-seller.

Collecting funky classics

If you want to collect in earnest, buy or borrow a history or directory of twentieth-century furniture design and read it from cover to cover. Scour junk shops and auctions for old leather armchairs, swivel chairs, stacking stools and chairs, smoked-glass coffee tables, old medicine cabinets, and office and school furniture. Hang around houses that are being refurbished and salvage old fixtures and fittings, or better still, consult builders working on warehouse conversions or apartment developments from former schools, hospitals, or municipal buildings. They may well be throwing out industrial fittings including lights, radiators, trolleys, blinds, and sanitaryware. Commerical refurbishments can also yield coveted '70s office furniture in unusual shades of orange, green, and beige. And remember, Eames chairs have graced many a school hall, airport lounge and public hall, so you never know what you might find.

It can sometimes be hard to tell whether an item you like is an 'original' or not, as so many modern classics have been in continuous (though slightly modified) production since they were first designed, and most don't carry special insignia. But if your heart is set on an early model, your best route is to do what museum curators try to do, and buy it directly from the person who bought it the first time, and has guarded it every since. Ask around, read the small advertisements in newspapers and magazines, or if you're desperate, advertise yourself. It is always worth browsing around shops selling twentieth-century classics as a starting point, although they can carry higher price tags. Once you have an idea of the going rate of items by your favorite designer you could try your luck at an auction, but be prepared to bid against keen collectors and traders.

If your decision is to buy new, go for stream-lined, curvilinear items in subtle colors that will still look good and stylish in years to come. Visit reputable chain stores whose furniture may be mass-produced but is still based on solid design values and aesthetic appeal. If you can afford it, buy your furniture from shops and galleries that play host to innovative designers. You may end up paying a little more today, but in turn you could pick an antique of tomorrow.

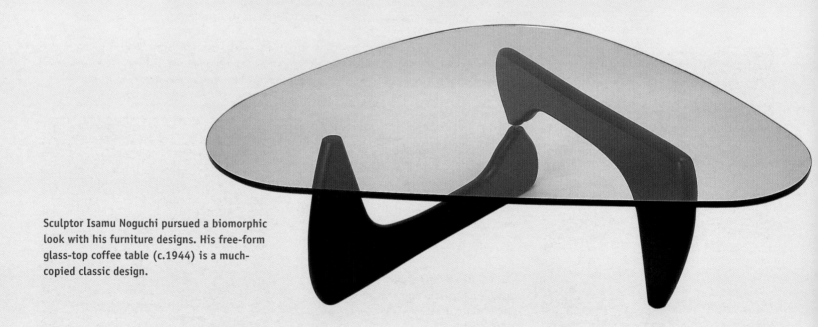

Sculptor Isamu Noguchi pursued a biomorphic look with his furniture designs. His free-form glass-top coffee table (c.1944) is a much-copied classic design.

ABOVE An ordinary table can be transformed with a new top made from zinc sheeting.

BELOW Industrial chic comes into the bedroom with a headboard made from scaffolding.

Customizing furniture

You could also experiment and customize furniture yourself. Old-fashioned haberdashers, hardware stores, stationers, "Asian" shops or stores, and art suppliers can be rich sources of unusual paints, finishes, trimmings, and papers.

Spray or paint table and chairs with silver or bronze for a sleek contemporary metallic look, or if you're handy with tools, use soft, flexible zinc sheeting (from large metal merchants) as splashbacks and covers for tables or chair seats.

Arm yourself with a staple gun and cover chairs, and stools with patterned and textured fabrics.

If you have an odd piece of wood or metal furniture that doesn't fit in with the rest of your room, paint it in a color a couple of shades deeper than your walls.

Vamp up old stools or chairs with a new seat made from the fluffiest, deepest fake fur or shag pile. (See pages 104–105 for details.)

Update old chairs or circular tables by removing the seat or center and replacing it with frosted, textured, or colored glass (toughened of course), cut to size by a glazier.

On smaller pieces of furniture such as cabinets, stools, or boxes, go for a fake '70s look with a coat of wood-effect paint.

Add your own handles in stainless steel, chrome, brass, or brightly-colored plastic.

RIGHT Office filing cabinets make smart storage units. Clean them up, give them a coat of paint if necessary, and add some typed labels.

A few practicalities

If you buy '50s or '60s fiberglass chairs, handle them carefully, as they are very brittle.

Be environmentally aware: some modern furniture is made from tropical hardwoods from endangered forests. Before you buy, even if the store claims the wood comes from managed forests, check that the supplier has a seal of approval from a reputable environmental organization.

If you are buying kitchen or dining chairs secondhand, measure the height of the seat from the floor and make sure it is compatible with your table, if you want to avoid knees on chins or, worse still, chins on tables!

Leather and plastic furniture is brilliantly stylish, and is a practical choice if you have young children, as it is durable and easy to clean, though spillages should be wiped off immediately as they can sometimes stain.

Take a tape measure with you when you're shopping for furniture, and make sure you know the dimensions of your rooms, doors, and hallways to avoid expensive mistakes.

fluffy seat cover

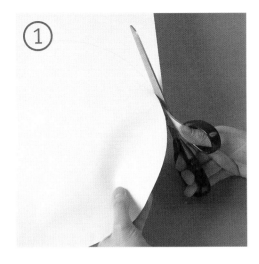

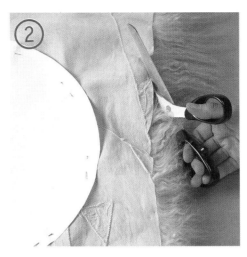

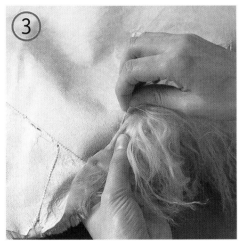

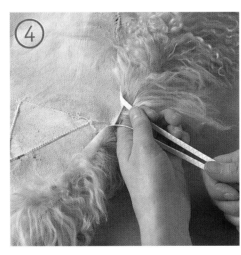

1. Make a template by placing some plain paper on top of the seat and drawing around the edge. Cut around the pencil outline. (The template does not have to be exact.)
2. Pin the template to the reverse side of the sheepskin and cut around it leaving a generous allowance for the thickness of the stool and the seam.
3. Hem all the way around the seat cover, leaving enough space for a carrier for the elastic and leave a gap to thread it through.
4. Cut a length of elastic that will fit snugly around the underside of the stool seat and attach the safety pin to one end. Thread it through the seam allowance (making sure you don't lose the other end). Pull the two ends tight, evenly distributing the gather of the skeepskin. Test the seat cover over the stool, and when satisfied that it's tight enough, tie the two ends in a secure knot and cut off any excess elastic.

Materials

Sugar pink Mongolian sheepskin
Thin elastic
Sewing thread and needle
Scissors
Plain paper
Pencil
Safety pin

TIPS I used a loose, thick-pile sheepskin, for the fluffiest varieties give the softest, most bouffant seat, but you could use any kind of fleece. If you plan to use the stool frequently, make sure you choose something hard-wearing, such as sheepskin. Check that the fleece you choose isn't prone to losing lots of fibers. If your stool seat doesn't already have padding, insert a thick layer of kapok under the fleece to give added height and bounce.

flexible living

Being funky means being mobile and flexible, ready to change and adapt your actions, mood, home, and style instantly in response to practical demands from your environment. So make the most of your living space, and look out for streamlined modular storage units and furniture, anything on wheels, storage cubes as well as freestanding vertical shelving. It is great to have an eclectic and vibrant home, and mixing the kitsch, the classic, and the old is positively de rigueur, but it doesn't mean displaying everything you've ever owned. As ever, it is a case of less is more, so unless you naturally incline toward the minimalist or live in a palace, selectivity and smart storage are paramount.

Maximize Your Living Space

Ever since Alvar Aalto pioneered his famous stacking stool back in the '20s we've been looking for design solutions to maximize our living space. Some eighty years later, more of us live in single-occupancy households than ever before, and city dwellers have pretty much gotten used to the limited environment of modern-day apartments. Our lifestyle has become all the more hectic, too: we get up, perhaps do some quick exercises, hurry off to work, dash home to prepare dinner, then off to bed. More and more people are working from home, and even for those who do travel to an office to work, there is often a need for a small home office area at home. For many people it is compact living—eating, sleeping, entertaining, working, and watching TV in just a few rooms. Life is busy, life is pressured, and life is full, and we need our homes to be arranged as efficiently as possible to make it run smoothly and painlessly, while at the same time keeping our sense of aesthetics razor sharp. So lose the surplus clutter, store (or better still, give away) what you don't need, and introduce furniture that is slim, pared-down, and above all, flexible.

LEFT We all need some version of a home office. By using strong, clean designs for your office furniture, you can set it up discreetly in the corner of the room, and the furniture pieces can be borrowed for other needs when needed.

One handy flexible basic is a good-quality sofa bed. It doesn't have to be huge, but it does need to be as good for sleeping on as for sitting, so look for a sturdy steel frame and a proper sprung mattress, plus a folding mechanism that is smooth and easy to operate. A foam-filled sofa bed will suffice, but bear in mind that the filling may become compacted and less comfortable after a year or two, and it will start to lose its shape.

A good alternative is a futon—but try lying on it before you buy one, as the firm surface is not to everyone's taste. If space is really tight, you can buy a futon as a "bed in a bag," which is simply a thin rolled-up mattress that stores in its own neat kit bag. And for extra sitting and sleeping arrangements that can be stored completely out of sight when not needed, buy an inflatable bed, armchair, or sofa—along with a sturdy pump.

Other living and storage necessities are catered for by a wide range of innovative furniture that combines great design with strong storage potential. They fall into four categories—multi-function, metamorphic, mobility and utility.

ABOVE An inflatable mattress deflates to almost no size and can be stored on a shelf. Some, like this model, come with their own rechargeable electric pump for blowing it up.

BELOW If your place is the size of a shoe box and friends still insist on sleeping over, this bed-in-a-bag futon is be the most compact way of accommodating them. It may not guarantee a perfect night's sleep, but it's affordable.

Multifunction

There is a huge range of dual-purpose furniture produced today that is well designed and stylish, and can allow you to keep the amount of furniture items in your home to a minimum, thus giving you a greater sense of space. Look for sofas and armchairs with book sleeves incorporated into the arms, low-slung tables with an internal shelf or mini-drawer, and blanket boxes and ottomans that double as seats, all of which will enable you to store small items out of sight.

BELOW A chic white leather couch can assume the appearance of a single bed, by removing the cushions for the back and arms.

RIGHT A shelf unit can be used to display objects or to hide them away in sturdy utilitarian boxes.

LEFT Storage cubes can be used individually as small tables for drinks and finger food, or they can be stacked and used as a bookshelf.

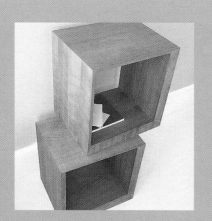

RIGHT A superb multifunctional unit is the trustworthy chest. You can use it as a table, a seat, and to store away the spare bedding and blankets for the sofa bed.

Metamorphic

The fun and the functional finds its best expression in furniture that can be taken apart and re-formed to make something else. Tables that can become seats, chaise-longues that can be transformed into beds, and other clever items can completely alter the look and role of a room. The unusual forms and arresting colors that characterize the new designs can add dramatic flair to your living area, while keeping the overall look clean and clutter-free.

RIGHT It looks like a pouffe can be used as a table and can be taken apart to make some wildly interesting floor seating.

ABOVE According to your needs, this piece of furniture can be either a table or a bench. Use the cushions as floor cushions.

RIGHT With a hinged back, this chair can be converted into a stool or small coffee table. With their simple design the stools can also be stacked in the corner, out of the way.

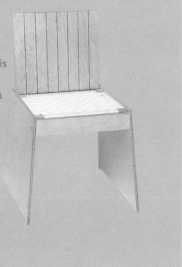

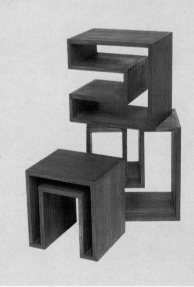

BELOW It's made from suede, it's the color of decadent dark chocolate, and it's totally gorgeous. The Cicero day bed can be lounged upon by day, and be transformed into a bed at night to impress your sleep-over guests.

ABOVE An ingenious take on the idea of nesting tables. The units can be stacked as one table, separated into three, placed upside down on top of each other to make an unusual bookcase, or on their sides as interesting sculptures.

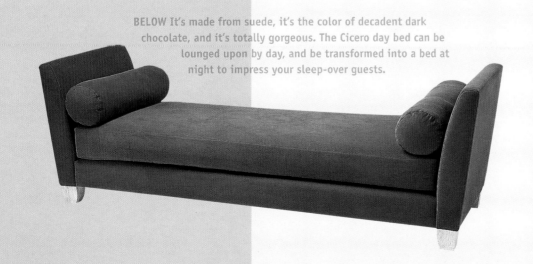

ABOVE This cabinet on wheels brings a modern look to freestanding furniture.

Mobility

Wheeled items in lightweight materials give you flexibility with style. Storage units can be wheeled against walls or moved into place as temporary screens to divide the room. Trolleys can be moved around the house or taken outside for serving drinks or food. Stacking stools and folding chairs can be stored in cupboards or against a wall and brought out for extra guests, as can beanbags and floor cushions.

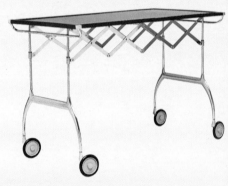

ABOVE The versatile trolley table adds a little industrial chic.

BELOW A tall shelf unit on castors can be used to display accessories, and can be moved into place as a room divider.

RIGHT A low coffee table can be moved around to suit your needs. If you own a bed on legs, you could store the table underneath the bed.

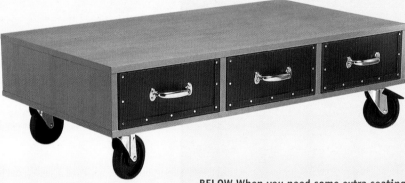

BELOW When you need some extra seating, bring out cool white floor cushions that will match any color scheme.

BELOW Get a couple of inflatable armchairs that can be moved from room to room.

Utility

Form follows function in the funky home. If something has been bought to serve a purpose, there is no reason why its utilitarian nature shouldn't be reflected in the design. Storage items can still look pleasing if they have simple lines and use quality materials with little unnecessary surface decoration.

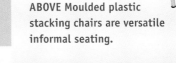

ABOVE Moulded plastic stacking chairs are versatile informal seating.

LEFT Tall slender shelving is perfect for slotting into recesses or tight spaces.

BELOW LEFT This coffee table can be extended and moved around depending on the shape of your room.

BELOW Translucent plastic drawers are undeniably stylish and allow you to see the items you are storing inside.

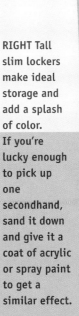

RIGHT Tall slim lockers make ideal storage and add a splash of color. If you're lucky enough to pick up one secondhand, sand it down and give it a coat of acrylic or spray paint to get a similar effect.

Hide it

It is one of those strange laws of physics that the number of possessions (read: clutter) you own always expands to fit the amount of space you live in. Under the bed, under the stairs, in the cellar, loft, garage, shed, on shelves, in cupboards, or simply in piles in a corner of the room, we all have "stuff" that we don't necessarily use on a daily basis but refuse to throw out on the grounds that "it may be useful one day."

Not everyone subscribes to a feng shui or minimalist lifestyle, but we can all afford to do a little sorting and pruning. After all, a heavy dose of clutter is horrible to look at and unsettling when it surrounds you. So discard as much of the surplus as you can bear to, and stack the remainder as neatly as you can in an attractive and imaginative storage facility. (See pages 116–117 for a simple storage box.) This will leave you more space to display your finest funky furniture and accessories, and for the important things in life, such as having friends around, doing yoga, or simply stretching your legs out a bit more.

If you can't zap it, then hide it behind a screen. You can buy wooden ones made out of MDF (medium density fiberboard) that comes ready to paint, or you could make one with four lengths of wood screwed together with small L-shaped brackets to form a rectangular frame. Cover with fabric tacked to the back or staple gunned in place. Make two, three, or four panels (use different-colored fabric if you like) and hinge them together. You could also mount the screens on castors.

ABOVE One minute it's a chair, the next it's a single bed. The leather *Convenio* sofa has considerably more style than an ordinary futon, and is easy to convert.

Create the illusion

When the room is small, a pair of compact two-seater sofas (one could be a sofa bed) is more balanced than a bulky three-seater option.

A plain daybed (narrow, no arms, no folding mechanism) covered with scatter cushions looks good enough to be a couch during the day, but converts without hassle into a bed at night. Store bedding underneath in a shallow box or wheeled drawer.

For clean, modern lines that help maximize all available space, go for reflective and clear materials such as steel, chrome, glass, and Perspex.

Choose streamlined furniture with slender legs that leave plenty of floor showing rather than squat, bulky items.

Make use of large mirrors to create the illusion of space, but don't go over the top or your house could end up looking like a fun fair.

Add castors to freestanding furniture so that it can be hidden under worktops if things get crowded.

When floorspace is tight, think vertical. Plywood boxes lined up in a vertical row look good. Leave them bare, or paint them the same color as the wall.

Make use of "dead" areas under the stairs, above a doorway, on the landing, or at the top of the hallway. Use them for storage, for a desk or to fit a cupboard. Invest in an extra large cupboard with a swivel-out shelf that can double as a work station for your computer.

customized boxes

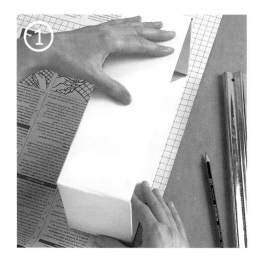

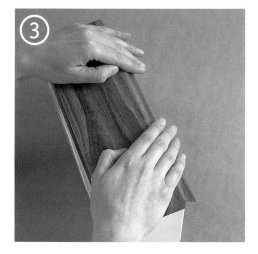

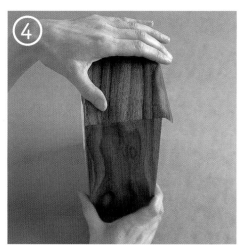

Materials

Shoe box
Scissors
Fablon or sticky-backed paper
Pencil
Ruler
Decoration

TIPS I used fake wood effect for this storage box for a groovy '70s effect, but any strong decorative paper will do. Make sure your shoe boxes are in good condition, as any defects will cause the paper to crease.

1 Using the grid on the reverse of the Fablon as a guide, place the box on its side and mark a piece to fit with a 3/4in (2cm) overlap at each of the four sides.

2 Cut out the paper.

3 Carefully peel away the back of the paper and stick down firmly on one side of the box, smoothing out air bubbles with your fingertips and pressing down the overlaps. Repeat for the other side of the box.

4 Mark out and cut a piece of Fablon that exactly fits the width of one end, with overlaps at the top and bottom. Peel away the back of the paper and stick down securely over one end, smoothing out air bubbles and pressing the overlap onto the bottom of the box and over the end. Repeat for the other end of the box.

5 For the lid: Mark and cut two pieces of Fablon for the two ends of the lid, with overlaps at all four sides. Peel away the back of the paper and stick down as before. Mark and cut a piece to cover across the width of the box with an overlap at the two sides and stick down as before. Add a decorative touch with a plastic fish, stickers, or photos.

accessories

You've painted your walls, chosen your furniture, and laid down your funky flooring, so now comes the fun part: the accessories that help a room leap to life and give it that stamp of individuality. Whatever you're into, this eclectic look can be home to almost any kind of decorative detail, from the downright outrageous to the ultra classic. So anything goes, but look especially for ephemera from the '50s, '60s, '70s. Even the '80s is cool. Slender wavy vases, abstract art, pop art (the real thing or contemporary imitations), big architectural plants and unusual flowers, bright plastic containers of all kinds, colorful glassware, high-energy gadgets and appliances, anything kitsch, homemade and customized pictures all have a place.

Displaying Accessories

Once you've put the basics into action, and your place is looking more like a cool pad, it's time to think about the finer details. Your much-loved accumulation of pictures, rugs, kitchen appliances, throws and office gadgets, cushions and ephemera are things that you have collected during the course of your life and make your home something you've created personally. But don't just collect for the sake of it: you only need around half the accessories you think you need. It's far more effective to display fewer but better-quality items. For the funky home, it is worth seeking out the rare and unusual.

When you're happy with your choice of accessories, it's nice to display them in a place where they are visually accessible. Don't get too obsessed about lining things up in rows or making everything the same height – funky is not about being finicky. On the other hand, some amount of organization can help.

Consider what items work well together in terms of color and shape. If you have a particular collection that takes pride of place in your heart, think about the best way to show it to advantage. For instance, football or baseball cards can be pegged onto thin wire with small clips and hung across a wall, or pinned together to make a lampshade. Large pictures can hang on their own to form a focal point, but small and medium pictures have more impact grouped together, especially if all their frames are

ABOVE & RIGHT Make your own pictures with a plain inexpensive frame and a little imagination. These show a row of plastic giraffe cocktail stirers; the other a child's hand print.

different. If the frames are identical you could hang them together in a line or square. Hang the largest picture first and arrange the others around it (experiment by arranging them on the floor first if you like) and keep the look fairly random—don't worry about getting the distance between each one exactly equal. If your walls aren't as straight as they could be, hanging them over a swathe of sheer fabric that hangs down to the floor helps hide faults. If your rooms are small, put larger pictures or groups in a hallway or landing so they don't over power the rest of the decor.

Large, wide picture frames with a tiny center or chunky box frames are stylish ways to display knick-knacks. Try an interesting leaf, a colorful, kitsch glass ornament, a fiery-red chile, a square of textured or handmade paper, one or two feathers on a background of tissue paper, or perhaps a row of three shapely shells. A vertical or horizontal row of wall-mounted wooden cubes is a good way to display items.

You don't have to invest in real art bought from galleries for huge sums of money. Try garage sales, auctions, charity shops and markets for affordable collectibles like '70s colored glassware, old posters, '50s lamps, slim-line '60s pottery or other unusual oddities. Or discover the next funky icon by haunting student graduation shows and local art exhibitions where you can often buy relatively inexpensive paintings, sculpture, ceramics, collages, and metalwork.

LEFT Storage cubes stacked off-center can be decorated with all kinds of bits and pieces, from colored glassware to your collection of dolls.

BELOW An old metal cabinet stripped of paint and polished is a great way to display a prized collection of CDs or alarm clocks – especially when it sits alongside Arne Jacobsen's classic *Ant* dining chair.

Accessorizing when cash is tight

Go for plain white crockery in a classic style. Source '70s-style geometric patterns or get something square and in a subtle color from flea markets or garage sales.

Change your light switches to shiny or pearlized metal.

Change handles
on doors, drawers, and light pulls.

Take a long hard look
at your lighting, and

invest in a few sleek new table lamps for an instant improvement.

Hide ugly bits and pieces of clutter in funky storage boxes or jars.

A small pile of interesting or pure white pebbles makes the ultimate cheap accessory, and sprayed in silver they are especially hip. Heap them on a window sill, a mantelpiece, in a clean fireplace or a clear glass vase.

Assortments of mismatched accessories such as picture frames, small vases, or candle holders that otherwise look odd or out of sync can be painted or sprayed all the same color. Pearlized or metallic paints, especially bronze and chrome, work well for this.

Customize plain glass shelves. Use a gift wrap motif as a template and place it underneath the glass shelf on a table. Copy the design using a small paintbrush dipped in water-based varnish. Spray etching spray over the shelf and it will become opaque, except for the varnished patterned areas.

TRY A CHIC INDUSTRIAL LOOK: measure the center panel of your kitchen cabinet doors and get a metal merchant to cut a piece of stainless steel the same size. Use a super strength adhesive to glue it on. Alternatively, you could use sheets of tough acrylicor Perspex in bright colors from a specialist supplier. Drill holes in each corner and simply screw them in.

Install a shelf above a radiator to protect walls from discoloration, and paint radiators the same color as your walls.

Customize plain lampshades or picture frames by sticking old sheets of music, maps, ordinary brown paper, or unusual gift wrap over the surface so they overlap, wait until the whole thing is dry, then apply a coat of clear water-based varnish. Or create an abstract pattern by splattering them randomly with emulsion paint, stick embroidered motifs over the surface with strong glue, or a length of gold bead fringing around the base (this works best on cylindrical lampshades).

Flower-arrange the modern way: paint a piece of board in different colors and attach glass test tubes with a strong adhesive. Half-fill them with water and add thin-stemmed blooms.

Make good use of old sweaters: turn them into one-off touchy-feely cushion covers. Simply put a cushion pad inside a roomy pullover, trim away the excess and sew a strongseam around the edges.

TURN UP THE HEAT with red-hot chile peppers and fake tomato plants(solanum) in old tins for a gutsy South American look.

If you don't like table cloths, make runners instead that go from one side of the table to the other, from deckchair decking or brilliantly colored paper.

If you haven't the time or the money for fresh flowers, fake it with silk: big bunches of overblown silk roses, artfully arranged Japanese cherry blossoms, or just two sprays of white orchids.

Immerse bright green marsh grass in a galvanized bucket.

Place mats can be funky: make your own from colorful or kitsch giftwrap overlaid with different images and then laminated, or pick a couple of your top photos and find a copy or printing shop that copies photos and make them into place mats. (You can do this for mouse pads too.)

Tie cutlery placings for table settings together with beads or sweets on elastic.

KITCHEN CUPBOARDS: Stick a rectangle of funky giftwrap exactly over the center panel of each cupboard door, and seal it with two coats of clear, quick-drying varnish.

Replace kitchen cupboard doors with safety glass.

Install some stainless steel shelving in your kitchen to complement shiny appliances.

Make splashbacks and table tops for the kitchen and bathroom from toughened safety glass, stainless steel or zinc.

Make transfers of your favorite images and stick them onto your cupboards. Seal with a coat of clear quick drying varnish. Take a photo of your favorite family member or pet, or just still life to a print of photographic services store that offers a copying service and magic the image onto a set of placemats.

Brightly colored or frosted glass wall tiles make funky place settings or coasters for drinks.

MAKE YOUR OWN PLACE SETTINGS: out of offcuts of wood and colored paper. (See pages 126-127.)

Buy paper labels, write the name of each guest and attach them to wine glasses with clothes pins.

Use luggage labels as place cards, tie decorative tape through the holes and write guests' names in gold or silver ink.

Place half a dozen thin, tapered candles at random in a boxy container filled with fine sand.

Place just the head of a gerbera or other wide-bloomed flower across each plate for a splash of color, or stand a single Michaelmas daisy in a plain glass by each person's place.

Wind colorful raffia around the stem of each wine glass and tie the ends in a bow.

Make simple table runners with white tissue paper, and stamp a design onto the surface with a rubber stamp dipped in metallic paint.

GO GREEN: There's nothing like a big, bold plant to add a touch of bio-drama to your living space – think big, bad and spiky.

If you have limited space, go for a quirky row of cacti lined up on a long, low table.
Go retro with a few Swiss cheese plants or self-cloning spider plants that are a throwback to the 70s. For something a little more restrained, small mounded or trailing plants closely planted in galvanized metal buckets are low maintenance and stylish.

Hide cheap terracotta pots inside interestingly textured raffia baskets or bright plastic laundry bins, or paint them indigo or silver.

Put sunflowers in a decorative tin, Chinese lanterns (*physalis*) in a hollowed-out butternut squash, ornamental cabbage leaves in a hessian-wrapped pot or artichoke flowers in a clear long-stemmed vase.

Knot together half a dozen vermilion amaryllis stalks with raffia and set in a chunky red glass vase, *ranunculus* in an opaque glass vase, pompom-shaped *alliums* in a silver container, or a couple of canna for an exotic touch of the jungle.

LEFT They're big, they're bad and they're funky, and they ought to be right there in your living room. With plants like these, you won't need much else as accessories.

RIGHT It may look like a UFO, but this is actually an inflatable fruit bowl. The ideal overseas funky Christmas present.

place settings

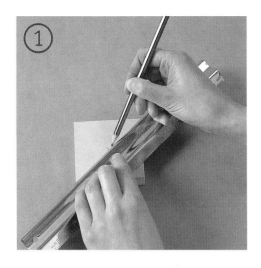

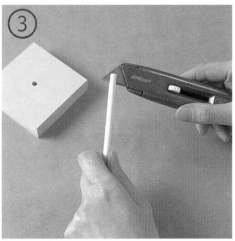

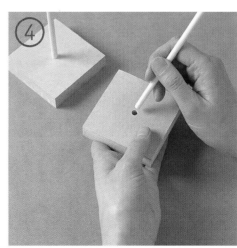

1   Mark the center of the wood with a small cross made by placing the ruler across the diagonals from corner to corner.
2   Drill a hole around ¹/₄in (¹/₂cm) deep.
3   With the Stanley knife, make a fine slit at the top of the dowel long enough to accommodate the card .
4   Push the dowel firmly into the hole until it is secure. Write and cut a colored label and tuck it in place at the top of the dowel. Use a different color for each setting.

Materials

Square of wood, approximately 3¹/₄in (8cm) across and ³/₄in (2cm) deep
Electric or hand drill with 6¹/₄ bit
5mm/³/₁₆in dowel approximately 6in (15cm) long
Sandpaper
Stanley knife or scalpel
Pencil
Colored card
Pen

TIPS Use different kinds of materials for the labels—transparent acrylic, shiny metallic, or textured paper. Experiment with different inks such as fluorescent and glittery. If you prefer something more decorative, paint the wood in brightly colored or metallic paint.

creating the look

Perhaps you're in the lucky position of having a totally blank canvas of a room, or more likely you have bits and pieces and a whole load of ideas about the way you'd like to get seriously funky. Either way, now is the time to step back and think about how all the different elements could work together. A little planning goes a long way, and even if you gave up drawing way back in high school, a few basic sketches or plans, plus paint chips, tear sheets, photos, and fabric swatches can help you get going and avoid heartbreaking mistakes.

The Look For You

Given the choice, many of us would probably begin our decorating efforts with a huge, totally empty room boasting vast windows, clean white walls, a superb fireplace, and gleaming beech floor, where all that's needed is the swipe of a paintbrush. Into this you could add a few choice pieces of furniture and a few treasured possessions. It's nice to fantasize about how you'd achieve that ultimate funky look given the perfect setting, but let's face it: not many of us have such gorgeously advantageous beginnings.

You're more likely to start off with an average-sized room with several items of furniture that you can't afford to change, or drab flooring that has to stay down for the forseeable future. Yet the worst thing you can do is compromise, using existing unsatisfactory furniture and accessories as the initial building blocks. If you're happy with what you have that's fabulous – you can build on that. But if you have a suspicion that Granny's cast-off couch in "autumn leaves" fabric isn't quite your thing, then stop right there. There is always a quick solution to problems such as these. Old sofas can have a dramatic shape to them, which may be in keeping with the funky ethos. You can easily cover faded or ugly fabrics with a throw (or sew two together if the item is a biggie) and piles of cushions.

LEFT Sugar pink is the perfect backdrop to a kitsch bedroom, in which a whole medley of different styles cohabit chaotically but happily. Sheepskin, raffia, feathers, and zebra prints add fun, fluff, and texture, while brazen floral curtains cling to the very edge of the taste scale.

RIGHT For a restrained retro look, the design of this room combines family heirlooms with bold designs in black leather and chrome.

BELOW Modern meets classic in this room that combines a few large, expensive pieces with smaller trinkets to fabulous effect, such as the intriguing modern light in the fireplace against the antique French mirror. The round table is a Charles Eames design.

Place a brightly colored rug over dingy carpets, paint over dark, unattractive wooden furniture, or rescue strangely colored curtains by dying them in the washing machine.

If you decide that something's truly beyond redemption, take it to your local recycling center or thrift store, as it may fit someone else's design scheme. With this in mind, when you're on a tight budget, it is always worth browsing through the second-hand shops.

The basics

First you need to decide on the overall look you want to achieve—whether it is kitsch, retro, or classic. This will help to bring a satisfying cohesion to your style. The pictures on pages 130, 131, and 132 should provide you with some interesting ideas. See which one appeals to you most.

Once you have a clear picture of how you want the room to look, you need to think about the dynamics: how people will move around it, whether you need to watch television, is it OK for social occasions; and the practicalities— where will you put the TV, VCR, and CD player, items of furniture; and how these will fit in with existing features such as alcoves, windows, fireplaces, and doors.

Once you've gotten rid of the thing you don't like or need, you can use whatever is left over as the basis for your room scheme, perhaps taking the color of a piece of furniture as a starting point for your wall, ceiling, and paint work colors. If you're not sure about combining colors, you could try one the following examples for instant success.

WARM

Warm colors are very easy to work and live with, and center around brown- and pink-based shades such as chocolate, coffee, burnt orange, almond, amber, and ochre, with sage green, soft grey, and sludgy blue as less obvious alternatives. Warm colors are ideal for rooms where the light is dull, and for the current mood of '70s styling.

aubergine & mustard

Wedgwood blue & milk chocolate

cranberry & ocean blue

COOL

Cool, pale colors are easy to coordinate and make for low-stress color scheming. They help you relax and are perfect for people who hate clutter and mess. Look for barely-there shades that are gentle on the eye such as watery blues, greys, aquas, chalky whites, and light beiges.

taupe & chalk white

sage & gooseberry

lilac & violet

REFRESHING

If it's an early morning wake-up call you're after, or a room to instill energy, go for fresh, clean colors with plenty of light in them. Be confident and combine fruity sorbet shades, lilac, raspberry, Caribbean turquoise, and zesty citrus colors.

strawberry ice cream & lime

orange sorbet & honeysuckle

turquoise & fuchsia

VIVID

If it's an impact you crave, choose deep, intense colors undiluted by much white pigment. Purple, scarlet, cornflower yellow, midnight blue, these are colors for confident decorators who reject neutrals in favor of drama and electricity.

flame & tangerine

sugar pink & scarlet

mulberry & Pacific blue

Layout

A simple-scale plan of the room should help you decide where to place things, and if space is a problem, the plan may reveal some space saving solutions.

SMALL NARROW ROOMS

A slim sofa against the longest wall and a couple of ottomans in front should maximize the space available, particularly if the ottomans can also be used for storage. Low, narrow shelving could sit directly opposite the sofa.

STRANGELY SHAPED ROOMS

Try placing a low table in the middle of the room with the seating grouped around informally rather than against the wall to minimize awkward dimensions.

SMALL ROOMS

Try placing the sofa far from the door to minimize its impact and allow floor space at the entrance to the room.

BOX-SHAPED ROOMS

Try two small sofas placed at right angles to each other with an additional armchair if there's room. If there are alcoves, use them for storage, and keep tables as low as possible.

Creating a focal point

Every room needs a focal point. Obviously, if there is something in the room already, such as a full-length window or an amazing fireplace, then that should be enough, but otherwise it is up to you to create it. Try an impressive floor lamp or ceiling light, or an oversize vase full of flowers, or let the furniture do the talking with a beautiful sculpted sofa or table. A stunning mirror also makes an easy focal point. If you have a plain one, you could try transforming it with glass etch spray with an original design so that it really grabs attention when people enter the room. (See pages 138–139 for details).

Ideally you should wait for the room to evolve rather than trying to make it work immediately, and you will find that a focal point may naturally emerge. The best thing about the funky look is its versatility, so try rearranging the furniture to create a new focal point every now and then.

Misuse, reuse, abuse.

Stash your kitchen in a tool trolley,

put industrial pallets on

floors and walls.

Be bold, be big,

use strong shape and color.

TOM DIXON, DESIGNER

Using a storyboard

You've decided on the look you are after, you've considered and planned the layout, bearing in mind your potential focal point, and you've thought about the color scheme. Now is the time to really narrow down your choice of paint and upholstery colors, the flooring, trimmings, and details. A storyboard is a really useful tool to help you experiment with different swatches and ideas, and visualize how they will work alongside each other.

Use a large piece of white card or mounting board to display paint chips, fabrics swatches, thread, trimming, piping, flooring, and worktop samples to see exactly how colors, finishes, and textures look together. Annotate your storyboard with notes on where you sourced the particular swatches and what area of furnishing or decorating they relate to.

If you are having trouble choosing between more than one color or finish, put both on the storyboard—the chances are that once you see everything together one choice will look better than another, and so you can eliminate as you go along. Use generously sized samples, roughly in proportion to their usage in the room, and keep introducing new ones until your instinct tells you its just right.

Steal other people's ideas by collecting tear sheets from home interiors magazines that appeal to you. If you're on a budget, try to be realistic – total up roughly how much you think it's all going to cost, then add about another 20 percent on top to cover unexpected contingencies.

The storyboard opposite outlines a modern, low-key scheme for a living room with a small kitchen area to one side, and centers around light, subtle colors, the minimum of pattern and paint with a soft sheen—all designed to maximize the light and make the space look larger. The funky element comes through in the choice of textures and materials. The color palette is limited but warm-hued, and is therefore easy on the eye and simple to work with.

Ready for change

The great thing about funky living is that it is all about going with the flow. So when your mood changes, you can change the furniture around; when you get bored with the colors, you can re-paint the walls; a couple of unexpected guests turn up, and you can alter the layout of the room to make it more sociable. It's all about achieving a fluid yet dynamic living environment. So spend time with a few key elements before you go all out for that final funky look.

UPHOLSTERY FABRICS

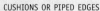

CUSHIONS OR PIPED EDGES

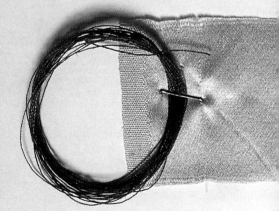

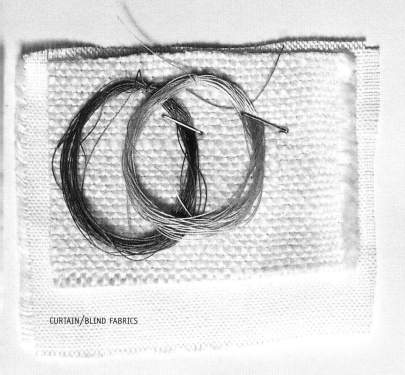

CURTAIN/BLIND FABRICS

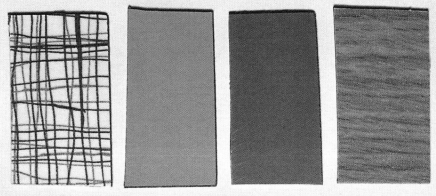

FORMICA SAMPLES FOR KITCHEN SURFACES

RUBBER FOR KITCHEN FLOOR

WALL 1

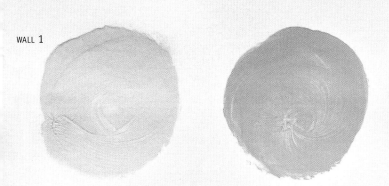

WALL EMULSION PAINTS

FLOOR PAINT COLORS

WALL 2

EDGING SAMPLES

acid-etched mirror

1. Place your mirror upside down onto a large sheet of paper and draw around it with a pencil.

2. Remove the mirror. Keeping within this outline, draw a random shape for the design to use as a stencil. Don't worry about making it too neat, the more curly and swirly the better. Cut out this shape. Working in a well-ventilated area, place the mirror right side up on sheets of newspaper. Spray mount the paper stencil, allow it to dry for a few seconds, and press it firmly into position on the surface of the mirror.

3. Holding the can of glass etching spray about 6in (15cm) away from the surface of the mirror, spray evenly the exposed area of the mirror. Give it two or three coats for a smooth finish. Allow it to dry.

4. Gently peel off the paper stencil. Any small marks can be easily removed with lighter fluid and a soft cloth.

Materials

Mirror
Glass etching spray
Spray Mount or Sellotape
Large sheet of paper
Scissors
Pencil
Newspaper

TIPS Glass etching spray is available at large hardware stores and artist's suppliers. Always read the instructions on the can before commencing. You can use the spray on lots of glass objects, including wine glasses, windows, bowls, vases, and paperweights, but the finish is not intended to be dishwasher-proof. If you decide to have a mirror cut to order for this project, ask for its edges to be beveled as this looks much neater.

Picture credits

All project photography, and the photographs on pages 42-43, 48, 74-75, 95, 136-137 were taken specially for the book by Chris Tubbs.

Other photography reproduced by kind permission:
Livingetc magazine, (listed by photographer):
44 Photography pp20, 22, 24 (bottom), 66, 70, 118; Peter Aprahamian pp26, 29, 31, 33, 39, 40 (left), 49, 64 (middle), 85 (bottom), 121 (bottom), 122, 128, 131 (bottom), 132; Graham Duddridge pp65, 94; Polly Eltes p106; Craig Knowles p120; Hannah Lewis p53; Tom Leighton pp55 (right), 76 (top right), 86, 103, 108; Jonathan Pilkington p96; Nick Pope p114; Ed Reeve pp7, 134; Tom Stewart pp6, 32, 61, 76 (bottom right), 79, 130; Chris Tubbs pp24 (top), 28, 30, 40 (right), 42, 46, 48, 58, 60 (bottom), 73 (left), 74, 76 (left), 84, 95, 136; Simon Watts pp38 (left), 121 (top); Verity Welstead pp50, 77; Polly Wreford pp3, 25, 52, 55 (left), 67, 82, 87, 88, 89, 131 (top).

Cut out photography by David Barrett, Mark Grimwade, Lee Hind, Moonlight Photographic, Bill Osment, PSC, Mel Yates

Colour magazine and Dulux pp36 and 41
   (photographer James Merrell)
Earl Carter/Belle/Arcaid p18.
Mathmos Ltd p63(left)
Matthew Bailey p115
Nick Crosbie p125
Paint Library p38 (top)
Pure Contemporary Design p100
Richard Waite/Arcaid p92
room magazine p85 (top) (photographer Richard Powers);

Any further inquiries regarding photography should be made in writing to the publishers.

Project index

Index

First published in the
United States of America in 1999
by UNIVERSE PUBLISHING
A Division of Rizzoli International Publications, Inc.
300 Park Avenue South
New York, NY 10010

99 00 01 02 / 10 9 8 7 6 5 4 3 2 1

Printed in Italy

Library of Congress Catalog
Card Number: **99-71289**